D1091600

Ryszard Kapuściński was born in eastern Poland in 1932. After studying Polish history at Warsaw University, he began work as a domestic reporter. Later, as a foreign correspondent for the Polish Press Agency (until 1981), he gained critical and popular praise for his coverage of civil wars, revolutions, and social conditions in the Third World. In Latin America, Africa and the Middle East, he ventured into the 'bush' – the word that has become his trademark – to search out hidden stories. In addition to his books on the Third World, Kapuściński has written about the Polish provinces and the Asian and Caucasian republics of the Soviet Union. He lives in Warsaw.

Ryszard Kapuściński

# THE EMPEROR

Translated from the Polish by
William R. Brand and
Katarzyna Mroczkowska-Brand

published by Pan Books

First published in Great Britain 1983 by Quartet Books Ltd
This Picador edition published 1984 by Pan Books Ltd,
Cavaye Place, London SW10 9PG
9 8 7 6 5 4 3 2
© Ryszard Kapuściński 1978
English translation © Ryszard Kapuściński 1983
ISBN 0 330 28373 1
Printed and bound in Great Britain by
Cox & Wyman Ltd, Reading

This book is sold subject to the condition that it
shall not, by way of trade or otherwise, be lent, re-sold,
hired out or otherwise circulated without the publisher's prior
consent in any form of binding or cover other than that in which
it is published and without a similar condition including this
condition being imposed on the subsequent purchaser

# CONTENTS

# THE THRONE

Forget about me—
The candle's been snuffed.
   (*Gypsy tango*)

Negus, our Negus,
Only you can save us
Our lines in the south
Have been caught in a rout
And to the north of Makale
All our tactics are folly.
Negus, our Negus,
Give me shot, give me powder.
   (*prewar Warsaw song*)

Observing the behavior of individual fowl in a henhouse, we
note that birds lower in rank are pecked by, and give way to,
birds of higher rank. In an ideal case, there exists a linear
order of rank with a top hen who pecks all the others. Those
in the middle ranks peck those below them but respect all
the hens above them. At the bottom there is a drudge who
has to take it from everyone.
   (Adolf Remane, *Vertebrates and Their Ways*)

Man will get used to anything, if only he reaches an
appropriate degree of submission.
   (C. G. Jung)

The DOLPHIN, desiring to sleep, floats atop the water;
having fallen asleep, he sinks slowly to the floor of the sea;
being awakened by striking the bottom, he rises again to the
surface. Having thus risen, he falls asleep again, descends
once more to the bottom, and revives himself anew in the
same fashion. He thus enjoys his rest in motion.
   (Benedykt Chmielowski, *The New Athens,
   or, An Academy Replete with All the Sciences*)

*I*n the evenings I listened to those who had known the Emperor's court. Once they had been people of the Palace or had enjoyed the right of admission there. Not many of them remained. Some had perished, shot by the firing squad. Some had escaped the country; others had been locked in the dungeons beneath the Palace, cast down from the chambers to the cellars. Some were hiding in the mountains or living disguised as monks in cloisters. Everyone was trying to survive in his own way, according to the possibilities open to him. Only a handful remained in Addis Ababa, where, apparently, it was easiest to outwit the authorities' vigilance.

I visited them after dark. I had to change cars and disguises. The Ethiopians are deeply distrustful and found it hard to believe in the sincerity of my intentions: I wanted to recapture the world that had been wiped away by the machine guns of the Fourth Division. Those machine guns are mounted next to the drivers' seats on American-made jeeps. They are manned by gunners whose profession is killing. In the back sits a soldier taking orders by radio. The jeeps are open, so the drivers, gunners, and radiomen wear dark motorcycle goggles under the brims of their helmets to protect themselves from the dust. You can't see their eyes, and their bristled ebony faces have no expression. These three-man crews know death so well that the drivers race their vehicles around suicidally, making abrupt high-speed turns, driving against the flow on one-way streets. Everything scatters when they come careening along. It's best to stay out of their range. Shouts and nervous screams blare amid crackles and squeals from the radio on the knees of the one in the back. You never can tell if one of the hoarse screams is an order to open fire. It's better to disappear. Better to duck into a side street and wait it out.

I penetrated the muddy alleys, making my way into houses that from the outside looked empty and abandoned. I

4

*was afraid. The houses were watched, and I was afraid of getting caught along with their inhabitants. Such a thing was possible, since they often made a sweep through a neighborhood or even a whole quarter of the town in search of weapons, subversive leaflets, or people from the old regime. All the houses were watching each other, spying on each other, sniffing each other out. This is civil war; this is what it's like. I sit down by the window, and immediately they say, "Somewhere else, sir, please. You're visible from the street. It would be easy to pick you off." A car passes, then stops. The sound of gunfire. Who was it? These? Those? And who, today, are "these," and who are the "those" who are against "these" just because they are "these"? The car drives off, accompanied by the barking of dogs. They bark all night. Addis Ababa is a dog city, full of pedigreed dogs running wild, vermin-eaten, with malaria and tangled hair.*

*They caution me again, needlessly: no addresses, no names, don't say that he's tall, that he's short, that he's skinny, that his forehead this or his hands that. Or that his eyes, or that his legs, or that his knees . . . There's nobody left to get down on your knees for.*

F.:

It was a small dog, a Japanese breed. His name was Lulu. He was allowed to sleep in the Emperor's great bed. During various ceremonies, he would run away from the Emperor's lap and pee on dignitaries' shoes. The august gentlemen were not allowed to flinch or make the slightest gesture when they felt their feet getting wet. I had to walk among the dignitaries and wipe the urine from their shoes with a satin cloth. This was my job for ten years.

## L. C.:

The Emperor slept in a roomy bed made of light walnut. He was so slight and frail that you couldn't see him—he was lost among the sheets. In old age, he became even smaller. He weighed fifty kilograms. He ate less and less, and he never drank alcohol. His knees stiffened up, and when he was alone he dragged his feet, swaying from side to side as if on stilts. But when he knew that someone was watching him, he forced a certain elasticity into his muscles, with great effort, so that he moved with dignity and his imperial silhouette remained ramrod-straight. Each step was a struggle between shuffling and dignity, between leaning and the vertical line. His Majesty never forgot about this infirmity of his old age, which he did not want to reveal lest it weaken the prestige and solemnity of the King of Kings. But we servants of the royal bedchamber, who saw his unguarded moments, knew how much the effort cost him.

He had the habit of sleeping little and rising early, when it was still dark outside. He treated sleep as a dire necessity that purposelessly robbed him of time he would rather have spent ruling or at Imperial functions. Sleep was a private, intimate interval in a life meant to be passed amid decorations and lights. That's why he woke up seeming discontented with having slept, impatient with the very fact of sleep. Only the subsequent activities of the day restored his inner balance. Let me add, however, that the Emperor never showed the slightest sign of irritation, nervousness, anger, rage, or frustration. It seemed that he never knew such states, that his nerves were cold and dead like steel, or that he had no nerves at all. It was an inborn characteristic that His Highness knew how to develop and perfect, following the principle that in politics nervousness signifies a weakness that encourages opponents and emboldens subordinates to make secret jokes. His Majesty knew that a joke is a dangerous form of opposition, and he kept his psyche in perfect order. He got up at four or five and, when going abroad on a visit, at three in the morning. Later, when things grew worse in our country, he traveled more often. Then, the only business of the Palace was to prepare the Emperor for new journeys. Upon waking, he rang the buzzer on his nightstand— the vigilant servants were waiting for the sound. The lights were turned on in the Palace. It was a signal to the Empire that His Supreme Majesty had begun a new day.

Y. M.:

The Emperor began his day by listening to informers' reports. The night breeds dangerous conspiracies, and Haile Selassie knew that what happens at night is more important than what happens during the day. During the day he kept his eye on everyone; at night that was impossible. For that reason, he attached great importance to the morning reports. And here I would like to make one thing clear: His Venerable Majesty was no reader. For him, neither the written nor the printed word existed; everything had to be relayed by word of mouth. His Majesty had had no schooling. His sole teacher—and that only during his childhood—was a French Jesuit, Monsignor Jerome, later Bishop of Harar and a friend of the poet Arthur Rimbaud. This cleric had no chance to inculcate the habit of reading in the Emperor, a task made all the more difficult, by the way, because Haile Selassie occupied responsible administrative positions from his boyhood and had no time for regular reading.

But I think there was more to it than a lack of time and habit. The custom of relating things by word of mouth had this advantage: if need be, the Emperor could say that a given dignitary had told him something quite different from what had really been said, and the latter could not defend himself, having no written proof. Thus the Emperor heard from his subordinates not what they told him, but what he thought should be said. His Venerable Highness had his ideas, and he would adjust to them all the signals that came from his surroundings. It was the same with writing, for our monarch not only never used his ability to read, but he also never wrote anything and never signed anything in his own hand. Though he ruled for half a century, not even those closest to him knew what his signature looked like.

During the Emperor's hours of official functions, the Minister of the Pen always stood at hand and took down all the Emperor's orders and instructions. Let me say that during working audiences His Majesty spoke very softly, barely moving his lips. The Minister of the Pen, standing half a step from the throne, had to bend his ear close to the Imperial lips in order to hear and write down the Imperial decisions. Furthermore, the Emperor's words were usually unclear and ambiguous, especially when he did not want to take a definite stand on a matter that required his opinion. One had to admire the Emperor's dexterity. When asked by a dignitary for the Imperial decision, he would not answer straight out, but would rather speak in a voice so quiet that it reached only the Minister of the Pen, who moved his ear as close as a microphone. The minister transcribed his ruler's scant and foggy mutterings. All the rest was interpretation, and that was a matter for the minister, who passed down the decision in writing.

The Minister of the Pen was the Emperor's closest confidant and enjoyed enormous power. From the secret cabala of the monarch's words he could construct any decision that he wished. If a move by the Emperor dazzled everyone with its accuracy and wisdom, it was one more proof that God's Chosen One was infallible. On the other hand, if from some corner the breeze carried rumors of discontent to the monarch's ear, he could blame it all on the minister's stupidity.

And so the minister was the most hated personality in the court. Public opinion, convinced of His Venerable Highness's wisdom and goodness, blamed the minister for any thoughtless or malicious decisions, of which there were many. True, the servants whispered about why Haile Selassie didn't replace the minister, but in the Palace questions were always asked from top to bottom, and never vice versa. When the first question was asked in a direction opposite to the customary one, it was a signal that the revolution had begun.

But I'm getting ahead of myself and must go back to the moment when the Emperor appears on the Palace steps in the morning and sets out for his early walk. He enters the park. This is when Solomon Kedir, the head of the Palace spies, approaches and gives his report. The Emperor walks along the avenue and Kedir stays a step behind him, talking all the while. Who met whom, where, and what they talked about. Against whom they are forming alliances. Whether or not one could call it a conspiracy. Kedir also reports on the work of the military cryptography department. This department, part of Kedir's office, decodes the communications that pass among the divisions—it's good to be sure that no subversive thoughts are hatching there. His Distinguished Highness asks no questions, makes no comments. He walks and listens. Sometimes he stops before the lions' cage to throw them a leg of veal that a servant has handed to him. He watches the lions' rapacity and smiles. Then he approaches the leopards, which are chained, and gives them ribs of beef. His Majesty has to be careful as he approaches the unpredictable beasts of prey. Finally he moves on, with Kedir behind continuing his report. At a certain moment His Highness bows his head, which is a signal for Kedir to move away. He bows and disappears down the avenue, never turning his back on the Emperor.

At this moment the waiting Minister of Industry and

Commerce, Makonen Habte-Wald, emerges from behind a tree. He falls in, a step behind the Emperor, and delivers his report. Makonen Habte-Wald keeps his own network of informers, both to satisfy a consuming passion for intrigue and to ingratiate himself with His Venerable Highness. On the basis of his information, he now briefs the Emperor on what happened last night. Again, His Majesty walks on, listening without questions or comments, keeping his hands behind his back. He approaches a flock of flamingos, but the shy birds scatter when he comes near. The Emperor smiles at the sight of creatures that refuse to obey him. At last, still walking, he nods his head; Habte-Wald falls silent and retreats backward, disappearing down the avenue.

Next, as if springing up from the ground, rises the hunched silhouette of the devoted confidant Asha Walde-Mikael. This dignitary supervises the government political police. He competes with Solomon Kedir's Palace intelligence service and battles fiercely against private informer networks like the one that Makonen Habte-Wald has at his disposal.

The occupation to which these people devoted themselves was hard and dangerous. They lived in fear of not reporting something in time and falling into disgrace, or of a competitor's reporting it better so that the Emperor would think, "Why did Solomon give me a feast today and Makonen only bring me leftovers? Did he say nothing because he didn't know, or did he hold his tongue because he belongs to the conspiracy?" Hadn't His Distinguished Highness often experienced, at cost to himself, betrayal by his most trusted allies? That's why the Emperor punished silence. On the other hand, incoherent streams of words tired and irritated the Imperial ear, so nervous loquaciousness was also a poor solution. Even the way these people looked told of the threat under which they lived. Tired, looking as if they hadn't slept, they acted under feverish stress, pursuing their victims in the stale air of hatred and fear that surrounded them all. They had no shield but the Emperor, and the Emperor could undo them with one wave of his hand. No, His Benevolent Majesty did not make their lives easy.

As I've mentioned, Haile Selassie never commented on or questioned the reports he received, during his morning walks, about the state of conspiracy in the Empire. But he knew what he was doing, as I shall show you. His Highness wanted to receive the reports in a pure state, because if he asked questions or expressed opinions the informant would obligingly adjust his report to meet the Emperor's expectations. Then the whole system of informing would collapse into subjectivity and fall prey to anyone's willfulness. The monarch would not know what was going on in the country and the Palace.

Finishing his walk, the Emperor listens to what was reported last night by Asha's people. He feeds the dogs and the black panther, and then he admires the anteater that he recently received as a gift from the president of Uganda. He nods his head and Asha walks away, bent over, wondering whether he said more or less than what was reported by his most fervent enemies—Solomon, the enemy of Makonen and Asha; and Makonen, the enemy of Asha and Solomon.

Haile Selassie finishes his walk alone. It grows light in the park; the fog thins out, and reflected sunlight glimmers on the lawns. The Emperor ponders. Now is the time to lay out strategies and tactics, to solve the puzzles of personality, to plan his next move on the chessboard of power. He thinks deeply about what was contained in the informants' reports. Little of importance; they usually report on each other. His Majesty has made mental notes of everything. His mind is a computer that retains every detail; even the smallest datum will be remembered. There was no personnel office in the Palace, no dossiers full of personal information. All this the Emperor carried in his mind, all the most important files about the elite. I see him now as he walks, stops, walks again, lifts his head upward as though absorbed in prayer. O God, save me from those who, crawling on their knees, hide a knife that they would like to sink into my back. But how can God help? All the people surrounding the Emperor are just like that—on their knees, and with knives. It's never comfortable on the summits. An icy wind always blows, and everyone crouches, watchful lest his neighbor hurl him down the precipice.

## T. K.-B.:

Dear friend, of course I remember. Wasn't it just yesterday? Yesterday, but a century ago. In this city, but on a planet that is now far away. How all these things get confused: times, places, the world broken in pieces, not to be glued back together again. Only the memory—that's the only remnant of life.

I spent a lot of time around the Emperor as a clerk in the Ministry of the Pen. We began work at eight, so that everything would be ready when the monarch arrived at nine. His Majesty lived in the New Palace, across from Africa Hall, and he performed his official duties in the Old Palace of the Emperor Menelik, built on a hill nearby. Our office was in the Old Palace, where most of the Imperial institutions were located, since Haile Selassie wanted to have everything within easy reach. He was brought there in one of the twenty-seven automobiles that made up his private fleet. He liked automobiles. He prized the Rolls-Royces for their dignified lines, but for a change he would also use the Mercedes-Benzes and the Lincoln Continentals. I'll remind you that our Emperor brought the first cars into Ethiopia, and he was always well-disposed toward the exponents of technical progress, whom unfortunately our traditional nation always disliked. Didn't our Emperor almost lose his power, and his life, when he brought the first airplane from Europe in the twenties? The simple airplane struck people as an invention of Satan, and in the courts of magnates there sprung up conspiracies against the Emperor as if he were a cabalist or a necromancer. His Revered Highness had to control ever more carefully his inclinations to act the pioneer until, in that stage of life when novelty holds little interest for an aged man, he almost gave them up.

And so at nine o'clock he would arrive at the Old Palace. Before the gate a crowd of subjects waited to try to hand petitions to the Emperor. This was theoretically the simplest way of seeking justice and charity in the Empire. Because our nation is illiterate, and justice is usually sought by the poor, people would go into debt for years to pay a clerk to write down their complaints and demands. There was also a problem of protocol, since custom required the humblest ones to kneel before the Emperor with their faces to the ground. How can anyone hand an envelope to a passing limousine from that posture? The problem was solved in the following manner. The vehicle would slow, the benevolent face of the monarch would appear behind the glass, and the security people from the next car would take some of the envelopes from the extended hands of the populace. Only some, for there was a whole thicket of these hands. If the mob crawled too close to the oncoming cars, the guards had to push back and shoo away the soliciting multitude, since security and the solemnity of majesty required that the procession be smooth and free of unexpected delays.

Now the vehicles drove up the ascending avenue and stopped in the Palace courtyard. Here, too, a crowd awaited the Emperor, but a different one from the rabble that had been furiously driven away by the select members of the Imperial Bodyguard. Those waiting in the courtyard to greet the Emperor were from the monarch's own circles. We all gathered early so as not to miss the Emperor's arrival, because that moment had a special significance for us. Everyone wanted very badly to be noticed by the Emperor. No, one didn't dream of special notice, with the Revered Emperor catching sight of you, coming up, and starting a conversation. No, nothing like that, I assure you. One wanted only the smallest, second-rate sort of attention, nothing that burdened the Emperor with any obligations. A passing notice, a fraction of a second, yet the sort of notice that later would make one tremble inside and overwhelm one with the triumphal thought "I have been noticed." What strength it gave afterward! What unlimited possibilities it created! Let's say that the Imperial gaze just grazes your face—just grazes! You could say that it was really nothing, but on the other hand, how could it really be nothing, when it did graze you? Immediately you feel the temperature of your face rise, and the blood rush to your head, and your heart beat harder. These are the best proofs that the eye of the Protector has touched you, but so what? These proofs are of no importance at the moment. More important is the process that might have taken place in His Majesty's memory. You see, it was known that His Majesty, not using his powers of reading and writing, had a phenomenally developed visual memory. On this gift of nature the owner of the face over which the Imperial gaze had passed could build his hopes. Because he could already count on some passing trace, even an indistinct trace, having imprinted itself in His Highness's memory.

Now, you had to maneuver in the crowd with such perseverance and determination, so squeeze yourself and worm through, so push, so jostle, so position your face, dispose and manipulate it in such a way, that the Emperor's glance, unwillingly and unknowingly, would notice, notice, notice. Then you waited for the moment to come when the Emperor would think, "Just a minute. I know that face, but I don't know the name." And let's say he would ask for the name. Only the name, but that's enough! Now the face and the name are joined, and a person comes into being, a ready candidate for nomination. Because the face alone —that's anonymous. The name alone—an abstraction. You have to materialize yourself, take on shape and form, gain distinctness.

Oh, that was the good fortune most longed for, but how difficult it was to realize! Because in the courtyard where the Emperor's retinue awaited him, there were tens, no, I say it without exaggeration, hundreds eager to push their faces forward. Face rubbed against face, the taller ones squelching down the shorter ones, the darker ones over-shadowing the lighter ones. Face despised face, the older ones moving in front of the younger ones, the weaker ones giving way to the stronger ones. Face hated face, the common ones clashing with the noble ones, the grasping ones against the weaklings. Face crushed face, but even the humiliated ones, the ones pushed away, the third-raters and the defeated ones, even those—from a certain distance imposed by the law of hierarchy, it's true—still moved toward the front, showing here and there from behind the first-rate, titled ones, if only as fragments: an ear, a piece of temple, a cheek or a jaw . . . just to be closer to the Emperor's eye! If His Benevolent Majesty wanted to capture with his glance the whole scene that opened before him when he stepped from his car, he would perceive that not only was a hundred-faced magma, at once humble and frenetic, rolling toward him, but also that, aside from the central, highly titled group, to the right and to the left, in front of him and behind him, far and even farther away, in the doors and the windows and on the paths, whole multitudes of lackeys, kitchen servants, janitors, gardeners, and policemen were pushing their faces forward to be noticed.

And His Majesty takes it all in. Does it surprise or amaze

him? I doubt it. His Majesty himself was once a part of the hundred-faced magma. Didn't he have to push his face forward in order to become the heir to the throne at the age of only twenty-four? And he had a hell of a lot of competition! A whole squadron of experienced notables was striving for the crown. But they were in a hurry, one cutting in front of the other, at each other's throats, trembling, impatient. Quickly, quickly, to the throne! His Peerless Majesty knew how to wait. And that is an all-important ability. Without that ability to wait, to realize humbly that the chance may come only after years of waiting, there is no politician. His Distinguished Majesty waited for ten years to become the heir to the throne, and then fourteen more years to become Emperor. In all, close to a quarter of a century of cautious but energetic striving for the crown. I say "cautious" because it was characteristic of His Majesty to be secretive, discreet, and silent. He knew the Palace. He knew that every wall had ears and that from behind every arras gazed eyes attentively scrutinizing him. So he had to be cunning and shrewd. First of all, one can't unmask oneself too early, showing the rapacity for power, because that galvanizes competitors, making them rise to combat. They will strike and destroy the one who has moved to the fore. No, one should walk in step for years, making sure not to spring ahead, waiting attentively for the right moment. In 1930 this game brought His Majesty the crown, which he kept for forty-four years.

When I showed a colleague what I was writing about Haile
Selassie, or rather about the court and its fall as described by the people who had frequented the chambers,
offices, and corridors of the Palace, he asked me whether I
had gone alone to visit the ones in hiding. Alone? That
would hardly have been possible. A white man, a foreigner
—none of them would have let you get a foot in the door
without powerful recommendations. And in any case, none
of them would want to confide in you (in general, it's hard
to get the Ethiopians to open up; they can be as silent as the
Chinese). How would you know where to look for them,
where they are, who they were, what they could tell you?

No, I was not alone. I had a guide.

Now that he is no longer alive, I can say his name: Teferra Gebrewold. I came to Addis Ababa in the middle of
May 1963. In a couple of days the presidents of independent
Africa were to meet there, and the Emperor was preparing
the city for the meeting. Addis Ababa was then a large village of a few hundred thousand inhabitants, situated on
hills, amid eucalyptus groves. Goats and cows grazed on the
lawns along the main street, Churchill Road, and cars had to
stop when nomads drove their herds of frightened camels
across the street. It was raining, and in the side streets vehicles spun their wheels in the gluey brown mud, digging
themselves in deeper until there were columns of nearly
submerged, immobilized automobiles.

The Emperor realized that the capital of Africa must look
more presentable, so he ordered the construction of several
modern buildings and the cleaning up of the more important
streets. Unfortunately, the construction dragged on endlessly, and when I saw the wooden scaffoldings scattered
about the city with workers on them, I remembered the scene
described by Evelyn Waugh (in They Were Still Dancing)
when he came to Addis Ababa to see the Emperor's coronation in 1930:

The whole town seemed still in a rudimentary stage of construction. At every corner were half-finished buildings; some had been already abandoned; on others, gangs of ragged Guraghi were at work. One afternoon I watched a number of them, twenty or thirty in all, under the surveillance of an Armenian contractor, at work clearing away the heaps of rubble and stone which encumbered the courtyard before the main door of the palace. The stuff had to be packed into wooden boxes swung between two poles, and emptied on a pile fifty yards away. Two men carried each load, which must have weighed very little more than an ordinary hod of bricks. A foreman circulated among them, carrying a long cane. When he was engaged elsewhere the work stopped altogether. The men did not sit down, chat, or relax in any way; they simply stood stock-still where they were, motionless as cows in a field, sometimes arrested with one small stone in their hands. When the foreman turned his attention towards them they began to move again, very deliberately, like figures in a slow-motion film; when he beat them they did not look round or remonstrate, but quickened their movements just perceptibly; when the blows ceased they lapsed into their original pace until, the foreman's back being turned, they again stopped completely.

*This time, great activity reigned on the main streets. Huge bulldozers rolled along the edges of the thoroughfares, destroying the first row of mud huts that had been abandoned the day before, when the police chased their occupants out of town. Next, brigades of masons built high walls to screen the remaining hovels from view. Other groups painted national designs on the wall. The city smelled of fresh concrete, paint, cooling asphalt, and the palm leaves with which the entry gates had been decorated.*
*The Emperor threw an imposing reception for the meet-*

ing of the presidents. Wine and caviar were flown in from Europe specially for the occasion. At a cost of twenty-five thousand dollars, Miriam Makeba was brought from Hollywood to serenade the leaders with Zulu songs after the feast. All told, more than three thousand people, divided hierarchically into upper and lower categories, were invited. Each category received invitations of a different color and chose from a different menu.

The reception took place in the Emperor's Old Palace. The guests passed long ranks of soldiers from the Imperial Guard, armed with sabers and halberds. From atop towers, spotlit trumpeters played the Emperor's fanfare. In the galleries, theatrical troupes performed scenes from the lives of past Emperors. From the balconies, girls in folk costumes showered the guests with flowers. The sky exploded in plumes of fireworks.

When the guests had been seated at tables in the great hall, fanfares rang out and the Emperor walked in with President Nasser of Egypt at his right hand. They formed an extraordinary pair: Nasser a tall, stocky, imperious man, his head thrust forward with his wide jaws set into a smile, and next to him the diminutive silhouette—frail, one could almost say—of Haile Selassie, worn by the years, with his thin, expressive face, his glistening, penetrating eyes. Behind them the remaining leaders entered in pairs. The audience rose; everyone was applauding. Ovations sounded for unity and the Emperor. Then the feast began. There was one dark-skinned waiter for every four guests. Out of excitement and nervousness, things were falling from the waiters' hands. The table setting was silver, in the old Harar style. Several tons of priceless antique silver lay on those tables. Some people slipped pieces of silverware into their pockets. One sneaked a fork, the next one a spoon.

Mountains of meat, fruit, fish, and cheese rose on the tables. Many-layered cakes dripped with sweet, colored *icing. Distinguished wines spread reflected colors and invigorating aromas. The music played on, and costumed clowns did somersaults to the delight of the carefree revelers. Time passed in conversation, laughter, consumption.*

*It was a splendid affair.*

*During these proceedings I needed to find a quiet place, but I didn't know where to look. I left the Great Chamber by a side door that led outside. It was a dark night, with a fine rain falling. A May rain, but a chilly one. A gentle slope led down from the door, and some distance below stood a poorly lit building without walls. A row of waiters stood in a line from the door to this building, passing dishes with leftovers from the banquet table. On those dishes a stream of bones, nibbled scraps, mashed vegetables, fish heads, and cut-away bits of meat flowed. I walked toward the building without walls, slipping on the mud and scattered bits of food.*

*I noticed that something on the other side was moving, shifting, murmuring, squishing, sighing, and smacking its lips. I turned the corner to have a closer look.*

*In the thick night, a crowd of barefoot beggars stood huddled together. The dishwashers working in the building threw leftovers to them. I watched the crowd devour the scraps, bones, and fish heads with laborious concentration. In the meticulous absorption of this eating there was an almost violent biological abandon—the satisfaction of hunger in anxiety and ecstasy.*

*From time to time the waiters would get held up, and the flow of dishes would stop. Then the crowd of beggars would relax as though someone had given them the order to stand at ease. People wiped their lips and straightened their muddy and food-stained rags. But soon the stream of dishes would start flowing again—because up there the great hogging, with smacking of lips and slurping, was going on, too*

—and the crowd would fall again to its blessed and eager labor of feeding.

I was getting soaked, so I returned to the Great Chamber, to the Imperial party. I looked at the silver and gold on the scarlet velvet, at President Kasavuba, at my neighbor, a certain Aye Mamlaye. I breathed in the scent of roses and incense, I listened to the suggestive Zulu song that Miriam Makeba was singing, I bowed to the Emperor (an absolute requirement of protocol), and I went home.

After the departure of the presidents (a hurried departure, since too long a stay abroad could lead to the loss of one's position), the Emperor invited us—the contingent of foreign correspondents assembled here on the occasion of the first conference of the leaders of African states—for breakfast. The news was brought to us at Africa Hall, where we spent days and nights in the hopeless and nerve-racking expectation of establishing contact with our capitals, by our local guardian, a section head from the Ministry of Information: none other than Teferra Gebrewold, a tall, handsome, usually silent and reserved Amhara. Now, however, he was excited. The striking thing was that every time he said the name of Haile Selassie, he bowed his head ceremoniously.

"This is wonderful news!" cried the Greco-Turko-Cypriot-Maltese Ivo Svarzini, who supposedly worked for the non-existent MIB Press Agency but really served as a spy for the Italian oil company ENI. "We'll be able to complain to the guy about how they've organized our communications here." I must add that the company of foreign correspondents at the farther corners of the globe consists of hardened, cynical men who have seen everything and lived through everything, and who are used to fighting a thousand obstacles that most people could never imagine, just to do their jobs. So nothing can excite them, and when they are exhausted *and angry they are likely to gripe even to an emperor about the lack of assistance they've received from local authorities. Yet even such people stop and think about their actions from time to time. Such a moment occurred now, when we noticed that at Svarzini's words Teferra had become pale and nervous, drooped forward, and begun muttering something of which we could understand only the conclusion: if we made such a report, the Emperor would have his head cut off. He repeated it over and over again. Our group split. I agitated for letting it ride and not having a man's life on our consciences. The majority felt the same way, and finally we decided to avoid the subject in our conversation with the Emperor. Teferra was listening to the discussion, and he should have been relieved at its outcome, but like all Amharas he was suspicious and distrustful, especially of foreigners. Depressed and downcast, he left us.*

*The next day, we were leaving the Emperor's presence, having received gifts of silver medallions bearing his arms. The master of ceremonies was leading us through a long corridor toward the front entrance. And there stood Teferra, against the wall in the posture of the accused before sentencing, with sweat covering his face. "Teferra!" shouted the amused Svarzini. "We praised you to the skies!" (as indeed we had). "You are going to be promoted," he added, and clapped Teferra on his trembling shoulders.*

*Afterward, for as long as he lived, I visited Teferra every time I was in Addis Ababa. Following the Emperor's deposition, he was active for some time. Fortunately for him, he had been kicked out of the Palace in the last months of Haile Selassie's reign. But he knew all the people from the Emperor's circle, and he was related to some of them by blood. As is characteristic of the Amharas, who are very conscious of their honor, he knew how to show gratitude. He always remembered that we had saved his neck. Soon after the Emperor was deposed, I met with Teferra in my room in the Hotel Ras. The town was swept up in the euphoria of the first months after the revolution. Noisy demonstrators flowed through the streets, some supporting the military government and others calling for its resignation; there were marches for agricultural reform, for bringing the old regime to justice, for distributing the Emperor's property among the poor. The feverish crowd filled the streets from early morning; fights broke out, and in the melee rocks were thrown. There in the room I told Teferra that I would like to find the Emperor's people. He was surprised, but he agreed to take it on himself. Our surreptitious expeditions began. We were a couple of collectors out to recover pictures doomed to destruction: we wanted to make an exhibition of the old art of governing.*

*At about that time the madness of the* fetasha, *which later grew to unprecedented proportions, broke out. We all fell victim to it—everyone, without regard to color, age, sex, or social status. Fetasha is the Amharic word for search. Suddenly, everyone started searching everyone else. From dawn to dusk, and around the clock, unceasingly, not stopping for breath. The revolution had divided people into camps, and the fighting began. There were no trenches or barricades, no clear lines of demarcation, and therefore anyone could be an enemy. The threatening atmosphere fed on the Amharas' pathological suspicion. To them, no man could be trusted, not even another Amhara. No one's word can be trusted, no one can be relied upon, because people's intentions are wicked and perverse; people are conspirators. Because the Amharic philosophy is pessimistic and sad, their eyes are sad but at the same time watchful and searing, their faces solemn, their features tense, and they can rarely bring themselves to smile.*

*All of them have weapons; they are in love with them. The wealthy had whole arsenals in their courts, and maintained private armies. In officers' apartments there were ar-*

senals, too. Machine guns, pistols, boxes of grenades. A couple of years ago, you could buy guns in the stores like any other merchandise. It sufficed to pay for them; nobody asked any questions. The arms of the plebeians were inferior and often quite old: flintlocks, breechloaders, muskets, shotguns, a whole museum to carry on one's back. Most of these antiques are useless because nobody produces ammunition for them any more. Thus, on the street market the bullet is often worth more than the gun. Bullets are the most valuable currency in that market, more in demand than dollars. After all, what is a dollar but paper? A bullet can save your life. Bullets make your weapons more significant, and that makes you more significant.

A man's life—what is that worth? Another man exists only to the degree that he stands in your way. Life doesn't mean much, but it's better to take it from the enemy before he has time to deliver a blow. All right (and also during the day) there is the sound of shooting, and later the dead lying in the streets. "Negus," I say to the driver, "they're shooting too much. It's not good." He remains silent, not answering. I don't know what he thinks. They have learned to draw their guns for any old reason and shoot.

To kill.

And perhaps it could be otherwise. Perhaps none of this is necessary. But they think differently. Their thoughts run not toward life but toward death. At first they talk quietly, then a quarrel breaks out, and the dispute ends in gunfire. Where do so much stubbornness, aggression, and hatred come from? All this without a moment's thought, without brakes, rolling over the edge of a cliff.

To get things under control, to disarm the opposition, the authorities order a complete fetasha, covering everyone. We are searched incessantly. On the street, in the car, in front of the house, in the house, in the street, in front of the post office, in front of an office building, going into the editor's *office, the movie theater, the church, in front of the bank, in front of the restaurant, in the marketplace, in the park. Anyone can search us, because we don't know who has the right and who hasn't, and asking only makes things worse. It's better to give in. Somebody's always searching us. Guys in rags with sticks, who don't say anything, but only stop us and hold out their arms, which is the signal for us to do the same: get ready to be searched. They take everything out of our briefcases and pockets, look at it, act surprised, screw up their faces, nod their heads, whisper advice to each other. They frisk us: back, stomach, legs, shoes. And then what? Nothing, we can go on, until the next spreading of arms, until the next fetasha. The next one might be only a few steps on, and the whole thing starts all over again. The searchers never give you an acquittal, a general clearance, absolution. Every few minutes, every few steps, we have to clear ourselves again.*

*The most tiring searchers are the ones we meet on the roads when traveling by bus. It happens scores of times. Everybody gets out, and the luggage is torn open and tossed around until it's in pieces. Every screw gets taken out and everything is spread out on the ground, and then it all gets browsed through slowly and thoroughly. We're searched, frisked, squeezed. Then the luggage, which has expanded like rising dough, all has to be stuffed back into the bus. At the next fetasha it all gets tossed out again, and clothes, tomatoes, and pots and pans get strewn and kicked around until the scene resembles an impromptu roadside bazaar. The searchers make the trip so miserable that halfway to anywhere you just want to stop the bus and get off, but what do you do then, in the middle of some field high up in mountains that are full of bandits?*

*Sometimes the searchers work over a whole quarter of the city. That's trouble. Then it's the army that does the fetasha looking for ammunition dumps, underground printing presses, and anarchists. During these operations you hear shots and see bodies. If anybody, no matter how innocent, gets in the way, he'll live through some difficult hours. He'll walk between the gun barrels with his hands over his head, waiting for his sentence. Usually, however, you have to deal with amateur searchers, and after a while you learn to put up with them. These lonesome searchers hold their own frisks, outside the general plan, lone wolves that they are. We're walking down the street when a stranger stops us and stretches out his arms. No way out of it; we have to spread ours and get ready. He'll give us a good feel, pluck around a little bit, give us a squeeze, and tell us we're free to go on. For a while he must have suspected us; now we're left in peace. We can forget him and go on. One of the guards in my hotel really enjoyed searching me. Sometimes when I was in a hurry and sprinted straight through the lobby and up the stairs to my room, he'd give chase. Before I could get through the door and lock him out, he'd get a foot in, wriggle in, and do a fetasha. I had fetasha dreams. A multitude of dark, dirty, eager, creeping, dancing, searching hands covered me, squeezing, plucking, tickling, threatening to throttle me, until I awoke in sweat. I couldn't get back to sleep until morning.*

*Despite these difficulties, I continued to go into the houses that were opened to me by Teferra. I listened to stories of the Emperor, stories that already seemed to come from another world.*

A. M.-M.:

As the keeper of the third door, I was the most important footman in the Audience Hall. The Hall had three sets of doors, and three footmen to open and close them, but I held the highest rank because the Emperor passed through my door. When His Most Exalted Majesty left the room, it was I who opened the door. It was an art to open the door at the right moment, the exact instant. To open the door too early would have been reprehensible, as if I were hurrying the Emperor out. If I opened it too late, on the other hand, His Sublime Highness would have to slow down, or perhaps even stop, which would detract from his lordly dignity, a dignity that meant getting around without collisions or obstacles.

G. S.-D.:

His Majesty spent the hour between nine and ten in the morning handing out assignments in the Audience Hall, and thus this time was called the Hour of Assignments. The Emperor would enter the Hall, where a row of waiting dignitaries, nominated for assignment, bowed humbly. His Majesty would take his place on the throne, and when he had seated himself I would slide a pillow under his feet. This had to be done like lightning so as not to leave Our Distinguished Monarch's legs hanging in the air for even a moment. We all know that His Highness was of small stature. At the same time, the dignity of the Imperial Office required that he be elevated above his subjects, even in a strictly physical sense. Thus the Imperial thrones had long legs and high seats, especially those left by Emperor Menelik, an exceptionally tall man. Therefore a contradiction arose between the necessity of a high throne and the figure of His Venerable Majesty, a contradiction most sensitive and troublesome precisely in the region of the legs, since it is difficult to imagine that an appropriate dignity can be maintained by a person whose legs are dangling in the air like those of a small child. The pillow solved this delicate and all-important conundrum.

I was His Most Virtuous Highness's pillow bearer for twenty-six years. I accompanied His Majesty on travels all around the world, and to tell the truth—I say it with pride —His Majesty could not go anywhere without me, since his dignity required that he always take his place on a throne, and he could not sit on a throne without a pillow, and I was the pillow bearer. I had mastered the special protocol of this specialty, and even possessed an extremely useful, expert knowledge: the height of various thrones. This allowed me quickly to choose a pillow of just the right size, so that a shocking ill fit, allowing a gap to appear between the pillow and the Emperor's shoes, would not occur. In my storeroom I had fifty-two pillows of various sizes, thicknesses, materials, and colors. I personally monitored their storage, constantly, so that fleas—the plague of our country—would not breed there, since the consequences of any such oversight could lead to a very unpleasant scandal.


T. L.:

My dear brother, the Hour of Assignments set the whole Palace trembling! For some, it was the trembling of joy, and a deeply sensuous delight; for others, well, it was the trembling of fear and catastrophe, since in that hour His Distinguished Majesty not only handed out prizes and distributed nominations and plums, but also punished, removed from office, and demoted. No, I've got it wrong. Really there was no division into happy and frightened ones: joy and fear simultaneously filled the heart of everyone summoned to the Audience Hall, since no one knew what awaited him there.

This uncertainty and obscurity with regard to our monarch's intentions caused the Palace to gossip incessantly and lose itself in supposition. The Palace divided itself into factions and coteries that fought incessant wars, weakening and destroying each other. That is exactly what His Benevolent Majesty wanted. Such a balance assured his blessed peace. If one of the coteries gained the upper hand, His Highness would quickly bestow favors on its opponents, restoring the balance that paralyzed usurpers. His Majesty played the keys—a black one and then a white one—and brought from the piano a harmonious melody soothing to his ears. Everyone gave in to such manipulation because the only reason for their existence was the Emperor's approbation, and if he withdrew it they would disappear from the Palace within the day, without a trace. No, they weren't anything on their own. They were visible to others only as long as the glamorous light of the Imperial crown shone upon them.

Haile Selassie was a constitutional Chosen One of God, and he could not associate himself with any faction (although he used one or another more than others), but if any one of the favored coteries went too far in its eagerness, the Emperor would scold or even formally condemn it. This was especially so for the extreme factions that our Emperor used to establish order. The Emperor's speeches were remarkably kindly, gentle, and comforting to the people, who had never heard his mouth form a harsh or angry word. And yet you cannot rule an Empire with kindness. Someone has to check opposing interests and protect the superior causes of Emperor, Palace, and State. That is what the extreme factions, the hard factions, were doing, but because they did not understand the Emperor's subtle intentions, they slipped into error—specifically the error of overdoing it. Desirous of His Majesty's approbation, they tried to introduce absolute order, whereas His Supreme Majesty wanted basic order with a margin of disorder on which his monarchical gentleness could exert itself. For this reason, the extremists' coterie encountered the ruler's scornful gaze when they tried to cross into that margin.

The three principal factions in the Palace were the aristocrats, the bureaucrats, and the so-called "personal people." The aristocrats, made up of great landowners and conservative in the extreme, grouped themselves mostly in the Crown Council, and their leader was Prince Kassa, who has since been executed. The bureaucrats, most enlightened and most progressive since some of them had a higher education, filled the ministries and the Imperial offices. The faction of "personal people" was a peculiarity of our regime, created by the Emperor himself. His Supreme Majesty, a partisan of a strong state and centralized power, had to lead a cunning and skillful fight against the aristocratic faction, which wanted to rule in the provinces and have a weak, pliable Emperor. But he could not fight the aristocracy with his own hands, so he always promoted into his circle, as representatives of the people, bright young men from the lowest orders, chosen from the lowest ranks of the plebeians, picked often on little more than a hunch from the mobs that surrounded His Majesty whenever he went among the people. These "personal people" of the Emperor, dragged straight from our desperate and miserable provinces into the salons of the highest courtiers—where they met the undisguised hatred of the long-established aristocrats—served the Emperor with an almost indescribable eagerness, indeed a passion, for they had quickly tasted the splendors of the Palace and the evident charms of power, and they knew that they had arrived there, come within reach of the highest state dignities, only through the will of His Highness. It was to them that the Emperor would entrust the positions requiring greatest confidence: the Ministry of the Pen, the Emperor's political police, and the superintendency of the Palace were manned by such people. They were the ones who would uncover intrigues and battle the mean, haughty opposition.

Listen here, Mr. Journalist, not only did the Emperor decide on all promotions, but he also communicated each one personally. He alone. He filled the posts at the summit of the hierarchy, and also its lower and middle levels. He appointed the postmasters, headmasters of schools, police constables, all the most ordinary office employees, estate managers, brewery directors, managers of hospitals and hotels—and, let me say it again, he chose them personally. They would be summoned to the Audience Hall for the Hour of Assignments and lined up there in an unending line, because it was a multitude, a multitude of people awaiting the Emperor's arrival. Each one approached the throne in turn, emotionally stirred, bowing submissively, listening to the Emperor's decision. Each would kiss the hand of his benefactor and retreat from the presence without turning his back, bowing all the time. The Emperor supervised even the lowliest assignment, because the source of power was not the state or any institution, but most personally His Benevolent Highness. How important a rule that was! A special human bond, constrained by the rules of hierarchy, but a bond nevertheless, was born from this moment spent with the Emperor, when he announced the assignment and gave his blessing, from which bond came the single principle by which His Majesty guided himself when raising people or casting them down: the principle of loyalty.

My friend, you could fill a library with the informants' reports that flowed into the Emperor's ears against the person closest to him, Walde Giyorgis, the Minister of the Pen. His was the most perverse, corrupt, repulsive personality ever to have been supported by the floors of our Palace. The very act of submitting a report against that man threatened one with the grimmest consequences. You can imagine how bad things must have been if, in spite of that, reports kept coming in. But His Highness's ear was always closed. Walde Giyorgis could do what he wanted, and his cruel self-indulgence knew no limits. And yet, blinded by his own arrogance and impunity, he once took part in the meeting of a conspiratorial faction about which the Palace security service informed His Sublime Majesty. His Majesty waited for Walde Giyorgis to inform him about this misdeed on his own, but Walde never so much as mentioned it—in other words, he violated the principle of loyalty. The next day His Majesty began the Hour of Assignments by dealing with his own Minister of the Pen, a man who almost shared power with His Exalted Majesty. From the second position in the state, Walde Giyorgis fell to the post of a minor functionary in a backward southern province. When he was informed of the assignment—just imagine the surprise and horror he must have been suppressing at that moment—he kissed the hand of his benefactor according to custom, withdrew backward, and left the Palace forever.

Or take a personality like Prince Imru. He was perhaps the most outstanding individual among the elite, a man deserving of the highest honors and positions. (But what of it, since, as I have already mentioned, His Majesty never made appointments on the basis of a person's talent, but always and exclusively on the basis of loyalty.) Nobody knows why or under what circumstances, but suddenly Prince Imru began to smell of reform, and without asking the Emperor's permission he gave some of his lands to the peasants. Thus, having kept something secret from the Emperor and acted by his own lights, in an irritating and even provocative way he violated the principle of loyalty. His Benevolent Highness, who had been preparing a supremely honorable office for the prince, had to exile him from the country for twenty years.

Here let me mention that His Majesty did not oppose reform. He always sympathized with progress and improvement. But he could not stand it when someone undertook reform on his own, first because that created a threat of anarchy and free choice, and second because it might create the impression of there being other charitable ones in the Empire besides His Magnanimous Highness. So, if a clever and astute minister wanted to carry out even the smallest reform in his own backyard, he would have to direct the case in such a way and so present it to His Majesty that it would irrefutably, in the commonly accepted fashion, seem that the gracious, concerned innovator and advocate of the reform was His Imperial Highness himself, even if in reality the Emperor did not quite understand what the reform was all about. But not all ministers have brains, do they? It sometimes happened that young people unacquainted with Palace tradition or those who, guided by their own ambition and also seeking popular esteem—as if the Emperor's esteem weren't the only one worth seeking!—tried independently to reform some little matter or other. As if they didn't know that by doing so they violated the principle of loyalty and buried not only themselves but also their reform, which without the Emperor's authorship didn't have a chance to see the light of day.

I'll come right out and say it: the King of Kings preferred bad ministers. And the King of Kings preferred them because he liked to appear in a favorable light by contrast. How could he show himself favorably if he were surrounded by good ministers? The people would be disoriented. Where would they look for help? On whose wisdom and kindness would they depend? Everyone would have been good and wise. What disorder would have broken out in the Empire then! Instead of one sun, fifty would be shining, and everyone would pay homage to a privately chosen planet. No, my dear friend, you cannot expose the people to such disastrous freedom. There can be only one sun. Such is the order of nature, and anything else is a heresy. But you can be sure that His Majesty shined by contrast. How imposingly and kindly he shone, so that our people had no doubts about who was the sun and who the shadow.


Z. T.:

At the moment of granting the assignment, His Majesty saw before him the bowed head of the one he was calling to an exalted position. But even the far-reaching gaze of His Most Unrivaled Majesty could not foresee what would happen afterward to that head. The head, which had been bobbing up and down in the Hall of Audiences, lifted itself high and stiffened into a strong, decisive shape as soon as it passed through the door. Yes, sir, the power of the Emperor's assignment was amazing. An ordinary head, which had moved in a nimble and unrestrained way, ready to turn, bow, and twist, became strangely limited as soon as it was annointed with the assignment. Now it could move in only two directions: down to the ground, in the presence of His Highness, and upward, in the presence of everyone else. Set on that vertical track, the head could no longer move freely. If you approached from the back and suddenly called, "Hey, sir," he wouldn't be able to turn his head in your direction, but instead would have to make a dignified stop and turn his whole body to face your voice.

Working as a protocol official in the Hall of Audiences, I noticed that, in general, assignment caused very basic physical changes in a man. This so fascinated me that I started to watch more closely. First, the whole figure of a man changes. What had been slender and trim-waisted now starts to become a square silhouette. It is a massive and solemn square: a symbol of the solemnity and weight of power. We can already see that this is not just anybody's silhouette, but that of visible dignity and responsibility. A slowing down of movements accompanies this change in the figure. A man who has been singled out by His Distinguished Majesty will not jump, run, frolic, or cut a caper. No. His step is solemn: he sets his feet firmly on the ground, bending his body slightly forward to show his determination to push through adversity, ordering precisely the movement of his hands so as to avoid nervous disorganized gesticulation. Furthermore, the facial features become solemn, almost stiffened, more worried and closed, but still capable of a momentary change to optimism or approval. All in all, however, they are set so as to create no possibility of psychological contact. One cannot relax, rest, or catch one's breath next to such a face. The gaze changes, too: its length and angle are altered. The gaze is trained on a completely unattainable point. In accordance with the laws of optics, an appointee cannot perceive us when we talk to him, since his focal point is well beyond us. We cannot be perceived because he looks obliquely, and, by a strange periscopic principle, even the shortest appointees look over our heads toward an unfathomable distance or in the direction of some particular, private thought. In any case, we feel that even though his thoughts may not be more profound, they are certainly more responsible. We realize that an attempt to convey our own thoughts would be senseless and petty. Therefore we fall silent. Nor is the Emperor's favorite eager to talk, since a change in speech is another postassignment symptom. Multiple monosyllables, grunts, clearings of the throat, meaningful pauses and changes of intonation, misty words, and a general air of having known everything better and for a longer time replace simple, full sentences. We therefore feel superfluous and leave. His head moves upward on its vertical track in a gesture of farewell.

As it happened, however, not only did His Benevolent Majesty advance people; unfortunately, upon perceiving disloyalty, he demoted people as well. If you will excuse my vulgar words, he kicked them into the street. Then one could observe an interesting phenomenon: upon contact with the street, the effects of promotion disappear. The physical changes reverse themselves, and the one who has hit the street returns to normal. He even manifests a certain exaggerated proclivity to fraternize, as if he wanted to sweep the whole affair under the rug, to wave it away and say, "Let's forget all that," as if it had been some illness not worth mentioning.

M.:

You ask me, friend, why, in the last days of the Emperor's reign, the plebeian Aklilu, a man with no official functions, exercised more power than the distinguished Prince Makonen, head of the government? Because the degree of power wielded by those in the Palace corresponded not to the hierarchy of positions, but rather to the frequency of access to His Worthy Majesty. That was our situation in the Palace. It was said that one was more important if one had the Emperor's ear more often. More often, and for longer. For that ear the lobbies fought their fiercest battles; the ear was the highest prize in the game. It was enough, though it was not easy, to get close to the all-powerful ear and whisper. Whisper, that's all. Get it in, let it stay there if only as a floating impression, a tiny seed. The time will come when the impression solidifies, the seed grows. Then we will gather the harvest. These were subtle maneuvers, demanding tact, because His Majesty, despite amazingly indefatigable energy and perseverance, was a human being with an ear that one could not overload and stuff up without causing irritation and an angry reaction. That's why access was limited, and the fight for a piece of the Emperor's ear never stopped.

The course of this fight was one of the liveliest topics of the gossiping Palace, and it echoed around the rabid town. For instance, Abeje Debalk, a low official in the Ministry of Information, enjoyed access four times a week and his boss only twice. People whom the Emperor trusted were scattered even among the lowest ranks, and yet because of their access they enjoyed powers that their ministers and the Crown Councillors couldn't dream of. Fascinating struggles were going on. The worthy general Abiye Abebe had access three times a week, and his adversary Kebede Gebre (both since shot) only once. But Gebre's lobby so managed things and so undermined Abebe's decrepit lobby that Abebe fell to two, and finally to only one, while Gebre, who had valuable international connections and had done well in the Congo, jumped to four times a week. In my best period, my friend, I could count on access once a month, even though others thought it was more. But even that was something, a significant position, because below those with access stood another whole hierarchy of those with no access at all, who had to go through one, two, or three others to reach the Emperor's ear. Even there you could see the claws: struggles, maneuvers, subterfuge. Oh, how everyone would bow to someone with a lot of access, even if he wasn't a minister. And one whose access was diminishing knew that His Majesty was pushing him down the slippery slope. I will add that, in relation to his modest size and pleasing form, His Supreme Majesty had ears of a large configuration.

I. B.:

I was the purse bearer to Aba Hanna Jema, the God-fearing confessor and treasurer to the Emperor. The two dignitaries were of the same age, of similar height, and they looked alike. To speak of a personal resemblance to His Distinguished Majesty, the Chosen One of God, sounds like a punishable impudence, but I am allowed such boldness in the case of Aba Hanna since the Emperor held him in the highest confidence. Aba Hanna's unlimited access to the throne proved the intimacy of this relationship. You could even call it continuous access. As keeper of the cashbox and confessor to our much-lamented monarch, Aba could look into the Imperial soul and the Imperial pocket—in other words, he could see the Imperial person in its dignified entirety. As his purse bearer, I always accompanied Aba in his fiscal activities, carrying behind him the bag of top-grade lambskin that those who destroyed everything later exhibited in the streets. I also took care of another bag, a large one that was filled with small coins on the eve of national holidays: the Emperor's birthday, the anniversary of his coronation, and the anniversary of his return from exile. On such occasions our august ruler went to the most crowded and lively quarter of Addis Ababa, Mercato, where on a specially constructed platform I would place the heavy, jingling bag from which His Benevolent Majesty would scoop the handfuls of coppers that he threw into the crowd of beggars and other such greedy riffraff. The rapacious mob would create such a hubbub, however, that this charitable action always had to end in a shower of police batons against the heads of the frenzied, pushy rabble. Saddened, His Highness would have to walk away from the platform. Often he was unable to empty even half the bag.


W. A.-N.:

. . . and so, having finished the Hour of Assignments, His Indefatigable Majesty would move on to the Golden Hall. Here began the Hour of the Cashbox. This hour came between ten and eleven in the morning. His Highness was accompanied by the saintly Aba Hanna, who in turn was assisted by his faithful bag bearer. Someone with good ears and a good nose could tell how the Palace rustled with money, smelled of it. But this called for special imagination and sensitivity, because money was not lying around the chambers, and His Merciful Highness had no inclination to spread packets of dollars among his favorites. No, His Highness cared little for that sort of thing.

Even though, dear friend, it might seem incomprehensible to you, not even Aba Hanna's little bag was a bottomless treasury. The masters of ceremony had to use all sorts of stratagems to prevent the Emperor from being embarrassed financially. I remember, for instance, how His Majesty paid the salaries of foreign engineers but showed no inclination to pay our own masons after the construction of the Imperial Palace called Genete Leul. These simple masons gathered in front of the Palace they had built and began asking for what was due them. The Supreme Master of Palace Ceremony appeared on the balcony and asked them to move to the rear of the Palace, where His Magnanimous Highness would shower them with money. The delighted crowd went around back to the indicated spot—which enabled His Supreme Majesty to leave unembarrassed through the front door and go to the Old Palace, where the court awaited him.

Wherever His Majesty went, the people showed their uncontrolled, insatiable greed. They asked now for bread, now for shoes, now for cattle, now for funds to build a road. His Majesty liked to visit the provinces, to give the plain people access to him, to learn of their troubles and console them with promises, to praise the humble and the hardworking and scold the lazy and the disobedient. But this predilection of His Majesty's drained the treasury, because the provinces had to be put in order first: swept, painted, the garbage buried, the flies thinned out, schools built, the children given uniforms, the municipal buildings remodeled, the flags sewn, and portraits of His Distinguished Highness painted. It wouldn't do if His Majesty appeared suddenly, unexpectedly, like some poor tax collector, or if he merely came into contact with life as it is. One can imagine the surprise and mortification of the local dignitaries. Their trembling! Their fear! Government can't work under threat, can it? Isn't government a convention, based on established rules?

Imagine His Worthy Highness's having the habit of arriving unannounced! Let's say our monarch is flying north, where everything has been prepared, the protocol spruced up, the ceremonies well rehearsed, the province gleaming like a mirror, and then suddenly in the airplane His Distinguished Highness beckons to the pilot and tells him, "Son, turn this plane around. Let's fly south." In the south, there is nothing! Nothing ready! The south is loafing around, a mess, in rags, black with flies. The governor is off in the capital, the dignitaries asleep, the police have slithered off to the villages to plunder the peasants. How badly His Benevolent Majesty would feel! What an affront to his dignity! And, not to mince words, how ridiculous! We have provinces where the people are depressingly savage, pagan, and naked; without instructions from the police they might do something that would offend His Highness's dignity. We have other provinces where the benighted peasantry would flee at the sight of the monarch. Just imagine it, friend. His Most Extraordinary Majesty steps off the airplane, and around him—nothing. Silent emptiness, deserted fields, and everywhere you look, not a living soul. No one to speak to, no one to console, no welcoming arch, not even a car. What can you do? How can you act? Set up the throne and roll out the carpet? That would only make it more ridiculous. The throne adds dignity only by contrast to the surrounding humility. This humility of the subjects creates the dignity of the throne and gives it meaning. Without the humility around it, the throne is only a decoration, an uncomfortable armchair with worn-out velvet and twisted springs. A throne in an empty desert—that would be disgraceful. Sit down on it? Wait for something to happen? Count on someone's showing up to render homage? What's more, there isn't even a car to get you to the nearest village to look for the viceroy. Our distinguished monarch knows who he is, but how to find him? So what remains for His Majesty to do? Look around the neighborhood, get back into the plane, and fly north after all, where everything waits in excitement and impatient readiness: the protocol, the ceremonies, the province like a mirror.

Is it surprising that in such circumstances His Benevolent Majesty did not sneak up on people? Let's say that he would surprise first one, then another, here and there. Today he would surprise the province of Bale, in a week the province of Tigre. And he notes: "loafing around, filthy, black with flies." He summons the provincial dignitaries to Addis Ababa for the Hour of Assignments, scolds them, and removes them from office. News of this spreads throughout the Empire, and what is the result? The result is that dignitaries stop doing everything except looking at the sky to see whether His Distinguished Highness is coming. The people waste away, the province declines, but all that is nothing compared to the fear of His Majesty's anger. And what's worse, because they feel uncertain and threatened, not knowing the hour or the day, united by common inconvenience and fear, they start murmuring, grimacing, grumbling, gossiping about the health of His Supreme Highness, and finally they start conspiring, inciting others to rebel, loafing, undermining what seems to them an uncharitable throne—oh, what an impudent thought—a throne that won't let them live. Therefore, in order to avoid such unrest in the Empire and to avoid the paralysis of government, His Highness introduced a happy compromise that brought peace to him and to the dignitaries. Nowadays, all those who destroyed the monarchy point out that in each province His Most Worthy Majesty maintained a Palace always ready for his arrival. It is true that some excesses were committed. For instance, a great Palace was constructed in the heart of the Ogaden Desert and maintained for years, fully staffed with servants and its pantry kept full, and His Indefatigable Majesty spent only one day there. But what if His Distinguished Majesty's itinerary were such that at some point he had to spend a night in the heart of the Desert? Wouldn't the Palace then prove itself indispensable? Unfortunately, our unenlightened people will never understand the Higher Reason that governs the actions of monarchs.

E.:

The Golden Hall, Mr. Kapuchitsky, the Hour of the Cashbox. Next to the Emperor stand the venerable Aba Hanna and, behind him, his purse bearer. At the other end of the Hall people are crowding in, apparently without order, but everyone remembers his place in the line. I can call it a crowd, since His Gracious Majesty received an endless number of subjects every day. When he stayed in Addis Ababa the Palace overflowed. It pulsated with exuberant life—though, naturally, a hierarchy was to be found here as well—rows of cars flowed through the courtyard, delegations crowded the corridors, ambassadors chatted in the antechambers, masters of ceremony rushed around with feverish eyes, the guard changed, messengers ran in with piles of papers, ministers dropped by, simply and modestly, like ordinary people. Hundreds of subjects tried to finagle their petitions or denunciations into the hands of the dignitaries. One could see the general staff, members of the

Crown Council, managers of Imperial estates, deputies—in other words, an excited and exhilarated crowd.

All this would disappear in an instant when His Distinguished Majesty would leave the capital on a visit abroad or to some province to lay a cornerstone, open a new road, or find out about the troubles of the people in order to encourage or console them. The Palace would immediately become empty and change into a replica of itself, a prop. The Palace servants did their laundry and strung their wash on clotheslines, the Palace children grazed their goats on the lawns, the masters of ceremony hung out in local bars, the guards would chain the gates shut and sleep under the trees. Then His Majesty would return, the fanfares would sound, and the Palace would come to life again.

In the Golden Hall there was always electricity in the air. One could feel the current flowing through the temples of those who had been summoned, making them quiver. Everyone knew the source of that current: the little bag of finest lambskin. People would approach His Benevolent Highness by turns, saying why they needed money. His Majesty would listen and ask questions. Here I must admit that His Highness was most meticulous about financial matters. Any expenditure, anywhere in the Empire, of more than ten dollars required his personal approval, and if a minister came to ask approval for spending only one dollar, he would be praised. To repair a minister's car—the Emperor's approval is needed. To replace a leaking pipe in the city—the Emperor's approval is needed. To buy sheets for a hotel—the Emperor must approve it.

How you should admire, my friend, the diligent thrift of His August Majesty, who spent most of his royal time checking accounts, listening to cost estimates, rejecting proposals, and brooding over human greed, cunning, and meddling. His lively curiosity, vigilance, and exemplary economy always attracted mention. He had a fiscal bent, and his Minister of Finance, Yelma Deresa, was counted among those with the most access to the Emperor. Yet to those in need, His Highness would stretch out a generous hand. Having listened as his questions were answered, His Charitable Majesty would inform the petitioner that his financial needs would be met. The delighted subject would make the deepest bow. His Magnanimous Highness would then turn his head in the direction of Aba Hanna and specify in a whisper the sum of money that the saintly nobleman was to take from the purse. Aba Hanna would plunge his hand into the bag, take out the money, put it into an envelope, and hand it to the lucky recipient. Bow after bow, backward, backward, shuffling his feet and stumbling, the fortunate one would leave.

And afterward, Mr. Kapuchitsky, one could unfortunately hear the cries of the wretched ingrate. Because in the envelope he would find only a fraction of the sum that—as the insatiable thieves always swore—had been promised to him by our generous Emperor. But what could he do? Go back? Hand in a petition? Accuse the dignitary closest to His Majesty's heart? No such thing was possible. What hatred therefore surrounded the God-fearing treasurer and confessor! Because, since general opinion dared not stain the dignity of His Highness, it reviled Aba Hanna as a miser and a cheat, who dipped so lightly into the bag and sifted so much with his thick fingers, who reached in with such disgust that the bag could have been full of poisonous reptiles, who knew the weight of money so well that he stuffed the envelope without looking and then gave the sign to shuffle away backward. That's why, when he was executed, I think no one but His Merciful Highness cried for him.

An empty envelope! Mr. Kapuchitsky, do you know what money means in a poor country? Money in a poor country and money in a rich country are two different things. In a rich country, money is a piece of paper with which you buy goods on the market. You are only a customer. Even a millionaire is only a customer. He may purchase more, but he remains a customer, nothing more. And in a poor country? In a poor country, money is a wonderful, thick hedge, dazzling and always blooming, which separates you from everything else. Through that hedge you do not see creeping poverty, you do not smell the stench of misery, and you do not hear the voices of the human dregs. But at the same time you know that all of that exists, and you feel proud because of your hedge. You have money; that means you have wings. You are the bird of paradise that everyone admires.

Can you imagine, for instance, a crowd gathering in Holland to look at a rich Dutchman? Or in Sweden, or in Australia? But in our land—yes. In our land, if a prince or count appears, the people run to see him. They will run to see a millionaire, and afterward they will go around and say, "I saw a millionaire." Money transforms your own country into an exotic land. Everything will start to astonish you— the way people live, the things they worry about, and you will say, "No, that's impossible." Because you will already belong to a different civilization. And you must know this law of culture: two civilizations cannot really know and understand one another well. You will start going deaf and blind. You will be content in your civilization surrounded by the hedge, but signals from the other civilization will be as incomprehensible to you as if they had been sent by the inhabitants of Venus. If you feel like it, you can become an explorer in your own country. You can become Columbus, Magellan, Livingstone. But I doubt that you will have such a desire. Such expeditions are very dangerous, and you are no madman, are you? You are already a man of your own civilization, and you will defend it and fight for it. You will water your own hedge. You are exactly the kind of gardener that the Emperor needs. You don't want to lose your feathers, and the Emperor needs people who have a lot to lose. Our kindly monarch would throw coppers to the poor, but to the people of the Palace he would make gifts of great worth. He would give them estates, land, peasants from whom they could collect taxes; he gave gold, titles, and capital.

Though everyone—if he proved his loyalty—could count on a bountiful gift, there were still continuous quarrels between lobbies, constant struggles for privileges, incessant grabbing, and all because of the needs of that bird of paradise that fills every man. His Most Extraordinary Majesty liked to watch this elbowing. He liked the people of the court to multiply their belongings, he liked their accounts to grow and their purses to swell. I don't remember His Magnanimous Highness's ever demoting someone and pressing his head to the cobblestones because of corruption. Let him enjoy his corruption, as long as he shows his loyalty! Thanks to his unequaled memory and also to the constant reports, our monarch knew exactly who had how much. But as long as his subject behaved loyally, he kept this knowledge to himself and never made use of it. But if he sensed even the slightest shadow of disloyalty, he would immediately confiscate everything and take the bird of paradise away from the embezzler. Thanks to that system of accountability, the King of Kings had everyone in his hand, and everyone knew it.

One case, though, was different. An outstanding patriot and a leader of the partisans in the war against Mussolini, Tekele Wolda Hawariat by name, was ill disposed toward the Emperor. He refused to accept graciously tendered gifts, refused special privileges, never showed any inclination to corruption. His Charitable Majesty had him imprisoned for many years, and then cut his head off.

G. H.-M.:

Even though I was a high ceremonial official, behind my back they called me His Distinguished Majesty's cuckoo. That was because a Swiss clock, from which a cuckoo would jump out to announce each hour, hung in the Emperor's office. I had the honor to fulfill a similar duty during the hours that His Highness devoted to his Imperial duties. When the time came for the Emperor, in accordance with official protocol, to pass from one activity to another, I would stand before him and bow several times. It was a signal to His Perspicacious Majesty that one hour was ending and that the time had come to start another.

The scoffers, who in any Palace like to make fun of their inferiors, would say jokingly that bowing was my only profession and even my sole reason for existing. Indeed, I had no other duty than bowing before His Distinguished Highness at a given moment. But I could have answered them— had my rank entitled me to such boldness—that my bows were of a functional and efficacious character and that they served a purpose of state, which is to say a superior purpose, whereas the court was full of nobles bowing whenever the occasion presented itself. And it was no superior purpose that made their necks so flexible, but only their desire to flatter, their servility, and their hope for gifts and promotions. I had to be careful not to let my own formal and functional bow get lost among those of the crowd. And I had to place myself where those pushy flatterers would not jostle me to the rear. After all, if our kindly monarch did not receive the established signal in time, he could fall into confusion and prolong his current activity at the expense of another equally important duty.

But, unfortunately, earnestness in performing my duty had little effect when it was time to finish the Hour of the Cashbox and begin the Hour of the Ministers. The Hour of the Ministers was devoted to Imperial matters, but who cares about Imperial matters when the treasure chest is open and the favorites and chosen ones are swarming around it like ants! No one wants to go away empty-handed, without a gift, without an envelope, without a promotion, without having cashed in. Sometimes His Highness would answer such greediness with a kindly scolding, but he never became angry, since he knew that it was because of the open purse that they pressed around him and served him more humbly. Our Emperor knew that one who is satiated will defend his own contentedness, and where else could one be satiated but in the Palace? Even the Emperor himself partook of this plenty, about which the destroyers of the Empire are now making so much noise.

I'll tell you, friend, that it got worse later on. The more the foundations of the Empire were crumbling, the more the chosen ones pressed forward to the cashbox. The more impudently the destroyers raised their heads, the more greedily the favorites stuffed their purses. The closer it got to the end, the more horrible was the grabbing and the unrestrained snatching. Instead, my friend, of applying himself to the tiller or the sails as the boat started to sink, each one of our magnates stuffed his bag and looked around for a comfortable lifeboat. Such fever broke out in the Palace, such scrambling for the purse, that even those who were not particularly interested in enriching themselves were dragged in, egged on, and so pressed upon that in the end, for their own peace and for dignity's sake, they also put something into their pockets. Because, my friend, things somehow got so turned around that it was decency to take and dishonor not to take. Not taking was seen as a frailty, some sort of laziness, some sort of pathetic and pitiable impotence. On the other hand, the one who had taken would go around looking as though he wanted to show off his masculinity, as if he wanted to say, full of self-assurance, "Kneel, you wretches!" It was all so topsy-turvy that I couldn't be blamed for tardily bringing the Hour of the Cashbox to an end so that His Benevolent Majesty could get on with the Hour of the Ministers.

P. H.-T.:

The Hour of the Ministers began at eleven o'clock and ended at noon. It was no trouble to call the ministers, since by custom these dignitaries stayed in the Palace all morning; various ambassadors often complained of being unable to visit a given minister in his office to take care of problems because the secretary would invariably say, "The minister has been summoned to the Emperor." In point of fact, His Gracious Highness liked to keep an eye on everyone, he liked to keep everyone within reach. A minister who stayed away from the Palace appeared in a bad light and never lasted long. But the ministers, God knows, didn't try to stay away. No one ever reached such a position without knowing the monarch's likings and trying assiduously to comply with them. Whoever wanted to climb the steps of the Palace had first of all to master the negative knowledge: what was forbidden to him and his subalterns, what was not to be said or written, what should not be done, what should not be overlooked or neglected. Only from such negative knowledge could positive knowledge be born—but that positive knowledge always remained obscure and worrisome, because no matter how well they knew what *not* to do, the Emperor's favorites ventured only with extreme caution and uncertainty into the area of propositions and postulates. There they would immediately look to His Distinguished Majesty, waiting to hear what he would say. And since His Majesty had the habit of being silent, waiting, and postponing things, they, too, were silent, waited, and postponed things.

Life in the Palace, however lively and feverish, was actually full of silence, waiting, and postponement. Each minister chose the corridors in which he thought he would have the greatest chance of meeting the distinguished monarch and making a bow. A minister who got the word that he had been denounced for disloyalty would show the greatest eagerness in this selection of itineraries. He would spend whole days trying to create an occasion for an obsequious meeting with His Highness in the Palace, in order to prove the falsity and maliciousness of the denunciation by constant attendance and radiant alacrity. His Most Extraordinary Majesty was in the habit of receiving each minister separately because a dignitary would then denounce his colleagues more boldly, giving the monarch a better insight into the operation of the Imperial apparatus. It is true that the minister being received at an audience preferred to talk about the disorders reigning in other departments rather than about those in his own, but precisely for this reason His Imperial Majesty, by talking to all the dignitaries, could put together an overall view. Anyway, it didn't matter if a given dignitary measured up or not, as long as he showed unshakable loyalty.

His Benevolent Highness would show favor to those ministers who were not distinguished by quick wits or perspicacity. He treated them as a stabilizing element in the life of the Empire, while he himself, as everyone knows, was always the champion of reform and progress. Reach, my dear friend, for the autobiography dictated by the Emperor in his last years, and you will be convinced of how His Valiant Highness fought against the barbarity and obscurantism that reigned in our country. [*He goes into the other room and returns with the London edition, published by Ullendorff, of* My Life and Ethiopia's Progress, *leafs through it, and continues talking.*] Here, for example, His Majesty mentions that at the beginning of his reign he forbade the customary punishment of cutting off hands and legs for even minor offenses. Next, he writes that he forbade the custom that a man who had been accused of murder—and this was only an accusation by the common people, because there were no courts—would have to be publicly executed by disembowelment, with the execution performed by the closest member of his family, so that, for example, a son would execute his father and a mother her son. To replace that custom, His Majesty instituted the office of state executioner, designated specific sites and procedures for executions, and stipulated that execution be only by shooting. Next, he purchased out of his own funds (a point that he emphasizes) the first two printing presses and recommended that the first newspaper in the history of the country begin publication. Next, he opened the first bank. Next, he introduced electricity to Ethiopia, first in the Palaces and then in other buildings. Next, he abolished the custom of shackling prisoners in chains and iron stocks. From then on, prisoners were watched over by guards paid from the Imperial treasury. Next, he promulgated a decree condemning the slave trade. He decided to end that trade by 1950. Next, he abolished by decree a method that we call *lebasha*, for the discovery of thieves. Medicine men would give a secret herb to small boys, who, dizzy, stupefied, and directed by supernatural forces, would go into a house and point out the thief. The one who had been pointed out, in accordance with tradition, had his hands and legs cut off. Just try to imagine, my friend, life in a country where, even though you are completely innocent of crime, you can at any moment have your hands and legs cut off. Yes, you're walking down the street when a stupefied child grabs your trouser leg, and immediately the crowd starts chopping. You're sitting at home eating a meal when a drunken boy rushes in; they drag you outside and chop you up in the courtyard. Only when you imagine such a life can you understand the profundity of the breakthroughs that His Distinguished Highness made.

And he kept on reforming: he abolished forced labor, he imported the first cars, he created a postal service. He retained public flogging as a punishment, but he denounced the *afarsata* method. If an offense were committed somewhere, the forces of order would surround the village or little town where it had occurred and starve the population until the guilty one was denounced. But the inhabitants all watched one another so that there would be no denunciation, because everybody feared that he would be denounced. And so, guarding each other this way, they would all die of hunger. This was the *afarsata* method. Our Emperor condemned such practices.

Unfortunately, driven by the desire for progress, His August Majesty committed a certain imprudence. Because there used to be no public schools or universities in our country, the Emperor began sending young people abroad to study. At some point in the past His Majesty himself directed this effort, choosing youngsters from good, loyal families. But later—ah, these modern times make your head throb—such pressure came to be applied, such pushing to go abroad, that His Benevolent Majesty gradually lost control over this craze that possessed our youth. More and more of these youngsters ventured to Europe or America for their studies, and—how else could it have ended?—after a few years the trouble started. Because, like a wizard, His Majesty breathed life into the supernatural destructive force that comparison of our country with others proved to be. These people would return home full of devious ideas, disloyal views, damaging plans, and unreasonable and disorderly projects. They would look at the Empire, put their heads in their hands, and cry, "Good God, how can anything like this exist?"

Here you have, my friend, another proof of the ingrati-

tude of youth. On the one hand so much care taken by His
Majesty to give them access to knowledge, and on the other
hand his reward in the form of shocking criticism, abusive
sulking, undermining, and rejection. It's easy to imagine the
bitterness with which these slanderers filled our monarch.
The worst thing is that these tyros, filled with fads unknown
to Ethiopia, brought into the Empire a certain unrest, an
unnecessary mobility, disorder, a desire for action against
authority, and it is here that the ministers who were not
distinguished by quick wits or perspicacity came to His Distinguished Highness's aid. Well, it wasn't deliberate help,
but spontaneous and unbidden, and yet how very important
for keeping peace in the Empire. Because it was enough for
one of those favorites of His Distinguished Highness to issue
a thoughtless decree. These young smart alecks see it, and
they immediately imagine some fatal result and come running to the rescue. They start trying to mend things,
straighten things out, patch things up and untangle them.
And so instead of using their energy to build their own vi-
sion of the future, instead of trying to put their irresponsible, destructive fantasies into action, our malcontents had
to roll up their sleeves and start untangling what the ministers had knotted up. And there's always a lot of work to
untangling! So they untangle and untangle, drenched in
sweat, wearing their nerves to shreds, running around,
patching things up here and there, and in all this rush and
overwork, in this whirlwind, their fantasies slowly evaporate
from their hot heads.

So now, my friend, let's look below the top levels. The
lower Imperial officials also cook up decrees, and the com-
moners stagger around, untangling. That is what the stabilizing role of His Majesty's favorites amounted to. These
courtiers, once they had driven the cultured, educated
dreamers and the stupid, uneducated common people to untangling, reduced all disloyal tendencies to zero—because

where could you find the energy for aspiration if all your energy has been spent on untangling? Thus, my friend, was maintained the blessed and amiable balance in the Empire over which His Exalted Majesty ruled so wisely and so kindly.

The Hour of the Ministers, nevertheless, caused anxiety among the humble ministers, since no one knew exactly why he was being summoned, and if His Majesty did not like what the minister said, or detected in it some reticence or beating around the bush, he could be replaced the next day during the Hour of Assignments. And in any case His Majesty was in the habit of constantly shuffling and reshuffling the ministers so that they would not get too comfortable or surround themselves with friends and relations. His Gracious Majesty wanted to reserve control of promotions to himself, and for that reason he looked with a malignant eye on any dignitary who tried to promote someone on the side. Such arbitrariness—immediately punished—threatened to upset the balance that His Distinguished Majesty had established; a bothersome disproportion would creep in and His Highness would have to worry about restoring the balance, instead of occupying himself with more important affairs.

B. K.-S.:

At noon, in my function as cloakroom attendant in the Imperial Court, I used to put upon the shoulders of His Most Extraordinary Highness a black, floor-length robe in which the monarch opened the Hour of the Supreme Court of Final Appeal, which lasted until one o'clock and was known in our language as *chelot*. His Majesty enjoyed this hour of justice, and when he was in the capital he never neglected his duty as a judge, even at the expense of other important duties. In accordance with tradition, His Majesty spent this hour standing, listening to cases and pronouncing sentences.

Our Imperial court was once a camp that moved from place to place and province to province in response to reports by the Emperor's secret service, whose task it was to determine in which region the harvest looked promising and where a bountiful birth of cattle had been noted. In such blessed places the itinerant capital of the Empire would arrive and the Imperial court would set up its innumerable tents. Afterward, when the grain and meat were gone, the Imperial court, directed by the ubiquitous secret service, would strike camp and move along to the next province on which an abundant harvest had been bestowed. Our modern capital, Addis Ababa, was the last stopping place of the Emperor Menelik's court. That illustrious Emperor ordered the establishment of the town and built the first of the three Palaces that adorn the city.

During the itinerant period, one of the tents, a black one, was a prison in which those suspected of particularly dangerous offenses were kept. In those days the Emperor, enclosed in a covered cage because no one was allowed to see his radiant face, presided over the Hour of Justice in front of the black tent. His Majesty of our days performed the function of supreme judge in a specially constructed building next to the main Palace. Standing on a platform, His Highness would hear the case as it was presented by counsel, and then pronounce his verdict. This was according to a procedure established three thousand years ago by the Israelite King Solomon, of whom His Most Exalted Majesty was a direct descendant—as established by constitutional law. Verdicts announced on the spot by the Emperor were final, without appeal, and if he imposed the death penalty it was carried out immediately. That was the punishment that fell on the heads of conspirators who impiously and without fear of anathema reached for power. But His Majesty's judg-

ment showed its benevolent side when by accident—
whether it was because of the guard's negligence or because
of some amazing cunning—some smallest of the small would
manage to appear before the face of the highest judge, beg-
ging for justice and denouncing some nobleman who had
victimized him. Then, His Benevolent Majesty would pronounce a sentence recommending the scolding of that dignitary, and the next day during the Hour of the Cashbox he
would order Aba Hanna to pay a generous amount to the
one who had been wronged.

M.:

At one o'clock His Distinguished Highness left the Old Palace and proceeded to the Anniversary Palace, his residence,
for dinner. The Emperor was accompanied by members of
his family and dignitaries invited for the occasion. The Old
Palace quickly emptied, silence filled the corridors, and the
guards fell into their midday slumber.

# IT'S COMING, IT'S COMING

One often observes a fear of falling in people. Yet even the best of competitive figure skaters can fall. We also meet with falls in everyday life. One has to learn how to fall painlessly. Of what does a painless fall consist? It is a directed fall, which is to say that after losing balance we direct the body so that it lands on the side where the least damage will be done. As we fall, we relax our muscles and roll up, protecting the head. A fall that follows in accordance with these principles is not dangerous. On the other hand, trying desperately to avoid a fall often causes a painful spill at the last moment, when there is no chance to prepare for it.

(Z. Osiński, W. Starosta, *Speed- and Figure-Skating*)

Too many laws are made, and too few examples given.
(Saint-Just)

There are public figures about whom nothing is known except that one should not offend them.
(Karl Kraus, *Aphorisms*)

Courtiers of all ages feel one great need: to speak in such a way that they do not say anything.
(Stendhal, *Racine and Shakespeare*)

They . . . have walked after vanity, and are become vain.
(Jeremiah)

You have sat long enough unless you had done more good.
(Cromwell, to the members of the Long Parliament)

F. U.-H.:

Yes, that was '60. A woeful year, my friend. A venomous maggot began to infest the robust and succulent fruit of our Empire, and everything took such a morbid and irreparable course that instead of juice, alas, the fruit oozed blood. Let the flags fly at half-mast and our heads droop sorrowfully. Let us lay our hands upon our hearts. Today we know that it was already the beginning of the end and that what came next was irreversibly fated.

I was then serving His Most Sublime Majesty as an officer in the Ministry of Ceremonies, Department of Processions. In only five years of zealous and unblemished service, I bore so many tribulations that every hair on my head turned white! This happened because each time our monarch was to go abroad or leave Addis Ababa to honor some province with his presence, savage competition broke out in the Palace for places in the traveling Imperial party. There were two rounds in this struggle. During the first, all our notables contended to be part of the Imperial party. In the second round, those who had triumphed in the preliminary stage strove for high and honorable places in the party. We officers at the very head of the procession, its first ranks, weren't involved in the struggle, since His Benevolent Highness chose those ranks himself, and an Imperial assistant passed his decrees to us by way of the master of Palace ceremonies. At the top of the list stood members of the royal family, the Crown Council, and luminaries that His Ineffable Highness had decided to keep within his royal view because he suspected that in his absence they might foment a conspiracy in the capital. Nor had we any problems defining the servants in the party: bodyguards, cooks, pillow bearers, valets, purse bearers, gift bearers, dogkeepers, throne bearers, lackeys, and maids. But between the top and the bottom of the list yawned an emptiness into which the favorites and the courtiers tried to insinuate themselves.

We ceremonial officers lived as if suspended between two great millstones, waiting for one of them to crush us. It was we who had to compile the list and send it on to our superiors. On us the crowd of favorites descended, attacking first with pleas and then with threats, first with laments and then with solemn vows of revenge; one asked for mercy while another proffered bribes, one promised heaps of gold while the next threatened to submit an informer's report about us. Patrons of the favorites dunned us constantly, and each recommended putting his chosen one on the list, backing up his words with threats. Yet who could blame these patrons? They themselves acted under pressure. All the while their underlings were making demands, and they themselves were jostling each other, for what a disgrace it would be for the patron who failed if another patron managed to place his favorite. Yes, the millstones began to turn and we ceremonial officers watched our hair turn white. Any one of these mighty patrons could crush us to a pulp, but was it our fault if the whole Empire could not fit into the traveling party?

And when everyone possible had been squeezed in and the list determined, pushing and undermining and elbowing began anew. Those who were lower were determined to rise. Number forty-three wanted to be twenty-sixth. Seventy-eight had an eye on thirty-two's place. Fifty-seven climbed to twenty-nine, sixty-seven went straight to thirty-four, forty-one pushed thirty out of the way, twenty-six was sure of being twenty-second, fifty-four gnawed at forty-six, sixty-three scratched his way to forty-nine, and always upward toward the top, without end. In the Palace there was agitation, obsession, running back and forth through the corridors. Coteries conferred, the court thought of nothing but the list until the word spread from office to salon to chamber that, yes, His Highness had heard the list, made wise and irrevocable corrections, and approved it. Now nothing could be changed and everyone knew his place. The chosen ones could be identified by their manner of walking and speaking, because on such an occasion a temporary hierarchy came into being alongside the hierarchy of access to the Emperor and the hierarchy of titles. Our Palace was a fabric of hierarchies and if you were slipping on one you could grab hold of another, and everyone found some satisfaction and reason to be proud of himself. Everyone spoke with admiration and jealousy of those who had made the list: "Look who's going!" Any dignitary distinguished several times in this way became a respected veteran.

All the machinations intensified greatly when His Highness was to visit a foreign country, from which one could return laden with presents and glorious decorations. In late 1960, our Emperor was preparing to visit Brazil. The court whispered that there would be abundant feasts, much buying, and the chance to stuff a bundle of cash into one's pockets. Thus a tournament for places began, and so fierce and grave was the jousting that no one noticed the malignant growth of a conspiracy in the very center of the Palace. But did no one catch the scent of it, my friend? Later it became evident that Makonen Habte-Wald had detected its stink early on, got hold of it, and reported it.

This Makonen, now deceased, was a strange personage. A minister, one of the select few, he had as much of a claim on the royal ear as he wanted, and yet he was a true favorite, a dignitary, who never thought of lining his own purse. His Majesty, even though he had little use for saints, pardoned his minister's bizarre weakness because he knew that Makonen forsook self-enrichment only to give his every thought to serving the Emperor. Makonen, my friend, was an ascetic of power, the Palace's great example of self-abnegation. He wore old suits, drove an old Volkswagen, and lived in an old house. His All-Dispensing Majesty liked Makonen's whole family, a humble clan who had climbed up from the dregs of society. He raised Makonen's brother Aklilu to the dignity of premier and made another brother, Akalu, a minister. Makonen himself was Minister of Industry and Commerce, but only rarely and unwillingly did he see to the duties of that station. He dedicated all his time and money to fostering his private network of informers. Makonen built a state within the state; he sowed his vassals in every institution, in offices, in the army, and in the police force. Day and night he reaped and winnowed his information, sleeping little, wearing himself out until he looked like a shadow. He was a penetrating man, but he penetrated quietly, like a mole, without theatricality, without rodomontade, gray, sour, hidden in the dusk, himself like the dusk. He tried to burrow deeply into the precincts of the competing spy networks, drawn by the scent of danger and treason, and—as we now know—rightly so. According to His Majesty's precept, if one sticks one's nose in deeply and well, it stinks everywhere. Yes . . .

**H**e tells me that in Makonen's cabinet, the private files of this fantastic dirt-collector, the folder with Germame Neway's name on it suddenly began to swell. The history of folders is strange, he says. Some linger for years on the shelf, thin and faded, like dried leaves. Closed, gathering dust, forgotten, they await the day when, untouched until that moment, they are finally torn up and thrown into the stove. These are the folders of loyal people who have led exemplary lives of devotion to the Emperor. Let's open the section marked "Activities": nothing negative. "Statements": not a single sheet of paper. And let's say there is one page, but on it, by order of the venerable Emperor, the minister has written fatina bere, which means "a slip of the pen," "an inkblot." This means that the Emperor considered the report a mere dry run by a young employee of Makonen, who hadn't yet learned whom one can denounce with confidence, and when. So there is a page, but it is invalidated, like a canceled invoice.

It can also happen that a folder which for years has remained thin and yellow comes to life at a certain moment, rises from the dead, starts getting fat. There is a well-known odor that comes from a place where an act of disloyalty has been committed. Makonen's nose is particularly sensitive to that odor. He begins to follow the scent, he watches, he increases his vigilance. Often the life of such a folder, which has begun to stir and gain weight, ends as abruptly as the life of its hero. They both disappear, he from the world and his folder from Makonen's cabinet.

There is a sort of inverse proportionality between the corpulence of folders and of people. He who wears himself out, loses weight, and wastes away in fighting against the Palace has a folder that grows fatter and fatter. On the other hand, he who plants himself with dignified loyalty at His Majesty's side grows fat with favors while his folder remains as thin as the membrane of a bladder. I mentioned that

64

*Makonen noticed the swelling of Germame Neway's folder.
Germame came from a loyal and noble family, and when he
finished school the benevolent monarch sent him on a schol-
arship to the United States, where he graduated from a university. He came back to the country at the age of thirty. He
had six years to live.*

A. W.:

Germame! Germame, Mr. Richard, was one of those disloyal
people who, upon returning to the Empire, threw up their
hands in exasperation. But they did that secretly. In public
they displayed loyalty, and in the Palace they said what was
expected of them. And His August Majesty—oh, how I reproach him for it today—let himself be taken in. When
Germame stood before him, His Compassionate Majesty
looked on him with a loving eye and made him governor of a
region in the southern province of Sidamo. The good soil
there yields rich coffee. Hearing of this appointment, everyone in the Palace said that Our Omnipotent Ruler was lay-
ing open the path to the highest honors for the young man.

Germame left with the Emperor's blessing, and at first
things were quiet. The proper thing for him to have done
was to wait patiently—patience is a cardinal virtue in the
Palace—for His Benevolent Majesty to summon him and
elevate him to the next grade. But forget that! After some
time, dignitaries from the province of Sidamo began to appear. They came and loitered around the Palace, circum-
spectly inquiring of their cousins and friends about whether
or not one could submit a denunciation of the governor. It is
a slippery business, Mr. Richard, to denounce one's superiors. One cannot do it haphazardly, without first buck-
ling on one's armor, because the governor might just have a

mighty patron in the Palace. The patron could fly into a rage, look upon the dignitaries as backstabbers, and perhaps even rebuke them. So the dignitaries started their denunciations in monosyllables, hints, whispers, but then more and more boldly (even if still informally), delicately, dropping hints in conversational lulls—that Germame took bribes and used them to build schools.

Now just imagine how worried these dignitaries must have been. After all, it was understandable that a governor accepted tributes; all the dignitaries accepted tributes. Power begat wealth, as it had since the beginning of the world. But the abnormality of it was this, that a governor should use these tributes to build schools. And the example at the top was a command to subordinates, which meant that all the dignitaries should give money for schools. Now just for a moment let us admit a base thought. Let us say that a second Germame springs up in a second province and starts to give away his bribes. Immediately we would have a mutiny of the dignitaries, protesting against this principle of giving away bribes. The result: the end of the Empire. A fine prospect—at first a few pennies, and finally the fall of the monarchy. Oh, no! The whole Palace cried out, "Oh, no!"

Yet the strange thing, Mr. Richard, was that His Most Venerable Highness said nothing. He heard it all, but he did not say a word. He kept silent, which meant that he was still giving Germame a chance. But Germame could no longer return to the road of obedience. Eventually, the dignitaries from Sidamo reappeared. They bore a report that Germame had gone too far: he had begun turning uncultivated acreage over to landless peasants, he was seizing private property by force. Germame had turned out to be a communist. Oh, what a grave matter, my good sir! Today he gives away wasteland, tomorrow the property of landowners, and he will finish with the Imperial holdings! Now His

Most Benevolent Majesty could hold his tongue no longer. Germame was summoned to the capital for the Hour of Assignments and sent down to be governor of Jijiga, where he couldn't give away land because the only inhabitants were nomads. During the ceremony, Germame committed an offense that should have awakened the utmost vigilance in His August Majesty: after hearing his appointment read, Germame failed to kiss the monarch's hand. Unfortunately . . .

It was then, he says, that Germame hatched his conspiracy. He hated Germame, and yet he also admired the man. There was something about him that drew people to him. Burning faith, a gift for persuasion, courage, decisiveness, keenness. Thanks to these characteristics he stood out against the gray, servile, fearful mass of yes-men and flatterers that filled the Palace. The first person Germame won over to his plan was his older brother, General Mengistu Neway, the chief of the Imperial Guard, an officer of fearless character and uncommon masculine good looks. Then the brothers gained the cooperation of the head of the Imperial Police, General Tsigue Dibou, the chief of Palace security, Colonel Workneh Gebayehu, and other members of the Emperor's inner circle. Working in strict secrecy, the conspirators set up a revolutionary council that numbered twenty-four people at the time of the coup. Officers of the Select Imperial Guard and the Palace security service made up the majority. Mengistu was the oldest at forty-four, but the younger Germame remained in command until the end.

The man who is telling me all this claims that Makonen started to suspect something and reported it to the Emperor. Then Haile Selassie summoned Colonel Workneh and asked him if it was true, but Workneh answered, "Not at all." Workneh was one of the Emperor's "personal people"—the monarch had lifted him straight up from the nether regions of society into the Palace chambers and had limitless confidence in him. He was probably the only man the Emperor really trusted. Suspicion of everyone is tiring; there has to be someone to trust, someone to feel at ease with. Furthermore, the Emperor discounted Makonen's reports because at the time he was directing his suspicions not at the Neway brothers, but at someone else: the dignitary Endelkachew, who lately seemed enervated, gloomy, anxious, drained of his usual spirit. Acting on his suspicions, the Emperor added

68

*Endelkachew to the traveling party so that he could keep an eye on him during the visit to Brazil.*

*My informant reminds me that the details of what happened next can be found in the testimony delivered by General Mengistu before the court martial. After the Emperor's departure, Mengistu handed out weapons to the officers of his Guard and instructed them to wait for further orders. It was Tuesday, the thirteenth of December. That evening, in the Empress Menen's residence, Haile Selassie's family and a group of high dignitaries gathered for supper. As they sat down at the table, Mengistu's messenger arrived with news that the Emperor had fallen ill during his trip, that he was dying, and that everyone should meet in the Palace to discuss the situation. When they had all assembled there, they were arrested. Meanwhile, officers of the Guard were arresting other dignitaries at their homes. But, as so often happens in a nervous situation, many dignitaries were forgotten. Several managed to escape from the city or to hide in friends' houses. Furthermore, the perpetrators of the coup were slow to cut off the telephones, and the Emperor's people had a chance to communicate and organize themselves. They were able to notify the Emperor that very night through the British Embassy. Haile Selassie broke off his visit and started for home, but without hurrying. He was giving the revolution time to collapse.*

*The following day, at noon, the Emperor's eldest son and the heir to the throne, Asfa Wossen, read a proclamation on the radio in the name of the rebels. Asfa Wossen was a weak, compliant man with no views of his own. There was animosity between him and his father, and it was whispered that the Emperor had doubts about whether Asfa was indeed his son. Something didn't quite fit in the dates of the Emperor's journeys and the time the Empress was blessed with her first child. Later, the forty-year-old son would try* to justify himself to his father by saying that the rebels had forced him at gunpoint to read the proclamation. "In the last years," Asfa Wossen read from what Germame had written for him, "stagnancy has reigned in Ethiopia. An atmosphere of discontent and disappointment has spread among peasants, merchants, office workers, in the army and the police, among students, all through society. There is no progress being made anywhere, in any quarter. This results from the fact that a handful of dignitaries have locked themselves into a course of egoism and nepotism, instead of working for the good of the whole community. The people of Ethiopia have waited for the day when poverty and backwardness would cease to be, but nothing has been achieved after innumerable promises. No other nation has borne so much in patience. . . ." Asfa Wossen announced that a People's Government had been formed, and he declared himself its head. But very few people had radios in those days, and the words of the proclamation drowned without a ripple. The city was quiet. Business thrived, the normal bustle and disorder reigned in the streets. Few people had heard anything, and those who had did not know what to think about the whole affair. For them it was a Palace matter, and the Palace had always been inaccessible, unreachable, impenetrable, beyond understanding, on a different planet.

That very day Haile Selassie flew to Monrovia, Liberia, and made radio contact with his son-in-law General Abiye Abebe, the governor of Eritrea. In the meantime this son-in-law had been conducting talks with a group of generals who, from the bases surrounding the capital, were preparing an assault on the rebels. Generals Merid Mengesha, Assefa Ayena, and Kebede Gebre, all relatives of the Emperor, led this group. My informant tells me that the coup was staged by the Guard and that there was sharp antagonism between the Guard and the army. The Guard was enlightened and well paid, the army ignorant and poor. Now the generals take advantage of this antagonism to hurl the army against the Guard. They tell the soldiers, "The Guard wants power so it can exploit you." What they say is cynical, but it convinces the army. The soldiers shout, "Let us perish for our Emperor!" Zeal drives the battalions about to go to their death.

On Thursday, the third day of the coup, the regiments loyal to the generals enter the suburbs of the capital. Indecision in the rebel camp. Mengistu gives no orders for defense; he doesn't want blood to be spilled. The city remains peaceful, with normal traffic in the streets. An airplane circles overhead dropping leaflets. The leaflets contain the text of the anathema that the Patriarch Basilios, head of the Church and friend of the Emperor, has pronounced on the rebels. The Emperor has already flown from Monrovia to Fort-Lamy, Chad. He receives a message from his son-in-law that he can fly on to Asmara. In Asmara things are peaceful and everyone is waiting submissively. But his DC-6 loses an engine. He decides to proceed on three engines. At noon Mengistu comes to the university to meet the students. He shows them a piece of dry bread. "This," he says, "is what we fed to the dignitaries today, so that they will know what our people live on. You must help us." Shooting breaks out in the city. The battle for Addis Ababa begins. Hundreds meet death in the streets.

Friday, the sixteenth of December, is the last day of the coup. Fighting between army and Guard regiments has been going on since morning. The revolutionary council defends itself in the Palace. The assault on the Palace begins in the afternoon. A battalion of tanks, commanded by the Emperor's son-in-law Captain Dereji Haile-Mariam, leads the assault. "Surrender, you dogs!" cries the captain from the turret of his tank. He falls, cut down by a burst of machine-gun fire. Shells explode inside the Palace. Smoke, flames, and a terrible din fill the corridors and chambers. Further de-

*fense is impossible. The rebels burst into the Green Chamber, where the dignitaries from the Emperor's circle have been held prisoner since Tuesday. The rebels open fire. Eighteen of the people who had been closest to the Emperor die. Now the leaders of the conspiracy and scattered regiments of the Guard leave the Palace grounds and withdraw from the city toward the eucalyptus woods on the Entoto Hills. Evening draws near. The airplane carrying the Emperor lands in Asmara.*

A. W.:

Oh, our loyal and humble people gave heartwarming proof of their devotion to His Most Praiseworthy Highness on that day of judgment, Mr. Richard. Because when the crushed infidels abandoned the Palace and fled to the neighboring woods, the populace, inspired by our Patriarch, set off in pursuit. Mind you, they had no tanks or cannon, so they grabbed whatever they could and joined the chase. Sticks, stones, pikes, daggers, everything went into action. The people of the streets, whom His Kindly Majesty used to shower with such generous alms, took furiously and hatefully to breaking the crazed heads of the calumniators and rebels who wanted to deprive them of God and prepare them for goodness knows what sort of life. If His Majesty were no longer there, who would give alms and fortifying words of comfort?

Following the bloody trail of the fugitives, the city dwellers drew village folk after them, so that you could see peasants with whatever weapons they could get their hands on—sticks, knives—cursing the slanderers. The peasants threw themselves into battle to avenge the affront to their generous ruler. Surrounded bands of the Guard defended themselves in the woods while their ammunition held out; later some gave themselves up, and others perished at the hands of the soldiers and the mob. Three thousand people, or perhaps as many as five thousand, ended up in prison, and twice that number died, to the joy of hyenas and jackals that came from far away to roam the woods in search of food. For a long time those woods laughed and howled all night long.

And those who had insulted His Unrivaled Majesty went straight to hell, my friend. General Dibou, for example, fell during the attack on the Palace and the mob hung his body in front of the gate of the First Division's base. Later it came out that after Colonel Workneh left the Palace, he was surrounded in the suburbs. They wanted to take him alive. But he didn't give in, Mr. Richard. He was shooting until the end. He even managed to kill a few soldiers. Then, when he was down to his last bullet, he put the barrel of the gun into his mouth, fired, and fell dead. They hung his body from a tree in front of Saint George's Cathedral. It may strain credulity, but His Highness could never bring himself to believe that Workneh had betrayed him. It was whispered afterward that even after many months the Emperor would summon servants to his bedroom late at night and ask them to call for the Colonel.

His Majesty flew into Addis Ababa on Saturday evening, when shooting could still be heard in the city and rebels were being executed in the squares. There was fatigue on our monarch's face, care and sorrow over the wrong that had been done him. He rode in his car, in the middle of a column of tanks and armored vehicles. All the citizens came out to pay humble and imploring homage. The whole city was kneeling on the ground, the people beating the sidewalks with their foreheads, and as I knelt in that crowd I heard moans, cries of woe, sighs, and wailing. No one dared look up into the face of our honorable monarch. At the gates of the Palace, Prince Kassa, who was hardly guilty, who had fought and had clean hands, kissed the Emperor's shoes. That same night His Unrivaled Highness ordered that his favorite lions be shot, because instead of defending the Palace they had admitted the traitors.

And now you ask about Germame. That evil spirit, together with his brother and a certain Captain Baye of the Imperial Guard, fled the city and remained in hiding for a week. They traveled only at night, for a price of five thousand dollars had immediately been put on their heads and everyone was looking for them, since that is a great deal of money. They tried to make their way south, probably intending to cross into Kenya. But after a week, as they sat hidden in the bushes—not having eaten for several days and fainting from thirst, afraid to show themselves in any village to get food and water—they were captured by peasants who had been beating the bush to find them. As Mengistu later testified, Germame decided to end it all right there. Germame, according to this survivor of the old regime, understood that he had gotten a step ahead of history, that he had walked more quickly than others, and he knew that someone who strides ahead of history with a gun in his hand is bound to perish. And he probably preferred that he and his fellow fugitives see to their own deaths. So when the peasants rushed forward to capture them, Germame shot Baye, then he shot his brother, and finally he shot himself.

The peasants thought they had lost their reward, because it was a reward for live capture, and they saw three corpses. However, only Germame and Baye were dead. Mengistu lay with his face covered with blood, but he was still alive. They rushed them to the capital and carried Mengistu into a hospital. His Majesty was informed of all this, and when he heard it he said that he wanted to see Germame's body. Accordingly, the corpse was brought to the Palace and thrown on the steps in front of the main entrance. His Majesty came out and stood for a long time, looking at the body that was lying there. He remained silent, gazing without saying a word. There were some others with him, and no one heard a sound. Then the Emperor turned, as if he had been startled, and went back into the main building, ordering his lackeys to close the door. Later I saw Germame's body hanging from a tree in front of Saint George's Cathedral. A crowd was standing around jeering at the traitors, hooting and raising vulgar cries. Mengistu was still alive. When he left the hospital, he faced a court martial. During the trial he behaved proudly and, contrary to Palace custom, showed neither any signs of humility nor any desire to obtain His Distinguished Majesty's pardon.

He said he wasn't afraid of death because when he decided to raise his head against injustice and attempt the coup, he expected to die. He said they had wanted to start a revolution, and since he would not live to see it he offered his blood so that the green tree of justice could sprout from it. They hanged him on the thirtieth of March, at dawn, in the main square. They hanged six other Guard officers along with him. He didn't look like himself at all. His brother's bullet had torn out his eye and shattered his whole face, which had grown a disheveled black beard. The remaining eye, under the pressure of the noose, squirted out of its socket.

*They* say that during the first days after the Emperor's return an unusual agitation reigned in the Palace. Charmen cleaned the floors, sanding soaked-in bloodstains from the parquet. Lackeys took down torn and partly burned curtains, trucks removed heaps of broken furniture and boxes full of empty shells, glaziers installed new windows and mirrors, masons replastered walls pockmarked ·by bullets. The smell of powder and smoke gradually disappeared. For a long time the ceremonial funerals of those who had preserved their loyalty to the end continued. At the same time the bodies of insurgents were buried at night in hidden, unknown places. Most of the dead had perished accidentally. Hundreds of gaping children, women on the way to market, and men going to work or idly sunning themselves had perished during the street fighting. Once the shooting had died down, the army patrolled the quiet city that only now, long after the fact, was beginning to feel the horror and the shock. They also say that later came weeks of fearsome arrests, exhaustive investigations, and brutal interrogations. Fear and uncertainty reigned. People whispered and gossiped, recalling details of the coup and embellishing them as their fantasy and courage allowed. Yet they embellished in secret, for all discussions of the latest events were officially banned, and the police, with whom one could not joke around even in the best of times (which these assuredly were not), became even more dangerous and efficient than usual in the effort to clear themselves of accusations that they had conspired. There was no lack of those willing to supply the police stations with additional terrified clients.

Everyone was waiting to see what the Emperor would do and declare next. On his return to the fearful, treason-tainted capital, he had expressed his pain and pity over the small group of lost sheep that had recklessly strayed from the herd and lost their way in a stony and bloodstained wilderness.

## G. O.-E.:

It had always been an act of punishable impudence to look
the Emperor straight in the eye, but now after what had
happened even the greatest daredevil in the Palace would
not have tried it. Everyone felt ashamed of having allowed
the conspiracy to occur and fearful of His Majesty's righ-
teous anger. And this half-frightened, half-shameful inabil-
ity to look each other in the eye showed in everyone's attitude
toward everyone else. Everyone succumbed to it. Because at
first no one knew where he stood, which is to say no one
knew whom the venerable Emperor would accept and whom
he would reject, whose loyalty he would confirm and whose
he wouldn't acknowledge, to whom he would give his ear
and to whom he would deny all access, and so everyone,
unsure of everyone else, preferred not to look anyone in the
eye. And so not looking, not seeing, watching the floor,
staring at the ceiling, inspecting the tips of one's shoes, and
gazing through windows into the distance were the order
of the day in the Palace. Now, if I started to look at
anyone, it would immediately awaken suspicious, ques-
tioning thoughts in him: Why is he watching me so carefully? What does he suspect me of? What does he have
against me? If I watch someone else, even in complete innocence or out of mere curiosity, he will not believe in my
innocence or curiosity or that I'm simply following the
human instinct to gawk. Instead, he will think me too eager,
suspicious, and to get the jump on me he will immediately
seek to clear himself. And how can he clear himself except
by dirtying the one he thought was out to dirty him?

Yes, looking was a provocation, it was blackmail, and
everyone was afraid to lift his eyes, afraid that somewhere—
in the air, in a corner, behind an arras, in a crack—he would
see a shining eye, like a dagger. And still the unanswered
questions—Who was guilty? Who had conspired?—hung

over the Palace like a thundercloud. To tell the truth, everyone was suspect, and rightly so, if three of the people closest to the Emperor, men of whom the Emperor had been so proud, in whom he had placed his greatest trust, could put a gun to his head. Think about it. Mengistu, Workneh, and Dibou belonged to the chosen handful who always had access to His August Majesty, and even, if the necessity arose, had the unique right to enter the bedchamber and wake him from his sleep. Imagine, my friend, the sort of feelings His Benevolent Majesty went to bed with from then on, never knowing whether he would wake up in the morning. Oh, what ignoble burdens and distresses come with power.

And how could we save ourselves from suspicion? There is no deliverance from suspicion! Every way of behaving, every action, only deepens the suspicions and sinks us the more. If we begin to justify ourselves, alas! Immediately we hear the question, "Why, son, are you rushing to justify yourself? There must be something on your conscience, something you would rather hide, that makes you want to justify yourself." Or if we decide to show an active attitude and goodwill, again we hear the comments, "Why is he showing off so much? He must want to hide his villainy, his shameful deeds. He's out to lie in ambush." Again it's bad, maybe worse. And, as I said, we were all under suspicion, all slandered, even though His Most Gracious Majesty said nothing directly or openly, not a word—but the accusation showed so in his eyes and his way of looking at his subjects that everyone crouched, fell to the ground, and thought in fear, "I am accused." The air became heavy, thick, the pressure low, discouraging, disabling, as if one's wings had been clipped, as if something had broken inside.

His Masterful Highness knew that after such a shock some people would start to become embittered, to grow gloomily silent, to lose enthusiasm, to give in to doubts and questions, to lose hope, to grumble, to surrender to weakness and decay—and that is why he started a purge in the Palace. It was not an instantaneous and complete purge, because His Majesty opposed impious and noisy violence, preferring an exchange in careful doses, thought out, which would keep the old residents in check and in constant fear while at the same time opening the Palace to new people. These were people who wanted to live well and make careers for themselves. They came from all over the land, directed to the Palace by the Emperor's trusted deputies. They had no close knowledge of the capital's aristocracy, but because of their low birth, crudeness, and clumsy thinking, they were held in contempt by the aristocracy and felt fear and aversion for the salons. Therefore they formed their own coterie, keeping close to the person of His Most Unparalleled Highness. The kindly grace of our venerable ruler made them drunk with a feeling of omnipotence, yet how dangerous that feeling of omnipotence could be in someone who wanted to disturb the evening atmosphere of an aristocratic salon or to irritate too long and too importunately the company gathered there! Oh, great wisdom and tact are needed to conquer a salon! Wisdom—or machine guns, which, my dear friend, you can see for yourself when you look at our tortured city today.

Gradually, these "personal people," our Emperor's chosen ones, began to fill the Palace offices, despite grumbling from members of the Crown Council, who considered the new favorites third-rate, falling far short of what ought to be required to serve the King of Kings. Yet this grumbling only proved the downright shameful naïveté of the Crown Council members, who saw weakness where His Highness saw strength, who could not comprehend the principle of strengthening by depreciating, and who remained oblivious to the fire and smoke raised only yesterday by those who had been elevated long ago and had proved themselves weak.

One important and useful characteristic of the new people

was that they had no past, had never taken part in conspiracies, trailed no bedraggled tails behind them, and had nothing shameful to hide in the lining of their clothes. Indeed, they didn't even know anything about conspiracies, and how were they going to find out about them if His Noble Majesty had forbidden the history of Ethiopia to be written? Too young, brought up in distant provinces, they could not know that in 1916 His Highness himself had come to power thanks to a conspiracy; that aided by European embassies, he had staged a coup and eliminated the legal heir to the throne, Lij Yasu. That in the face of the Italian invasion he had sworn publicly to spill his blood for Ethiopia and then, when the invaders marched in, had gone by boat to England and spent the war in the quiet little town of Bath. That later he had developed such a complex about the leaders of the partisans who had remained in the country to fight the Italians that when he returned to the throne he gradually eliminated them or shoved them aside, while granting favor to the collaborators. And that he had done away with, among others, the great commander Betwoded Negash, who came out against the Emperor and wanted to proclaim a republic in the 1950's. Many other events come to mind, but in the Palace it was forbidden to talk about them, and, as I said, the new people could not know about them and did not show much curiosity. And as they had no old connections, their only chance for survival was to keep themselves tied to the throne. Their only support: the Emperor himself. And thus His Most Extraordinary Majesty created a force that, during the last ten years of his reign, propped up the Imperial throne that Germame had undermined.

Z. S.-K.:

. . . and as the purge went on, every day when the Hour of Assignments—and therefore of demotions—drew near, we old Palace functionaries were overcome by shivering fits as we sat behind our desks. Everyone was trembling for his fate, ready to do anything to keep them from pulling that piece of furniture from under his elbows. During Mengistu's trial, fear reigned behind the desks, fear that the general would start accusing everyone of having been in on the conspiracy. Even very distant participation, even clandestine clapping, led one right to the noose. So when Mengistu pointed at no one, holding his tongue until the Day of Judgment, a winged sigh of relief arose from behind those desks. But a different fear immediately replaced the fear of the gallows: the fear of the purge, of personal destruction. His Most Benevolent Highness no longer hurled people into dungeons, but very simply sent them home from the Palace, and this sending home meant condemnation to oblivion. Until that moment you were a man of the Palace, a prominent figure, a leader, someone important, influential, respected, talked about, and listened to; all this gave one a feeling of existence, of presence in the world, of leading a full, important, useful life. Then His Highness summons you to the Hour of Assignments and sends you home forever. Everything disappears in a second. You stop existing. Nobody will mention you, nobody will put you forward or show you any respect. You may say the same words you said yesterday, but though yesterday people listened to them devoutly, today they don't pay any attention. On the street, people pass you with indifference, and you can already see that the smallest provincial functionary can tell you to go to hell. His Majesty has changed you to a weak, defenseless child and thrown you to a pack of jackals. Good luck!

And then, God forbid, what if they start investigating,

sniffing around, poking into things? Although sometimes I think it's better after all if they start to sniff around. Because if they start to sniff around, at least you can come back into existence, if only in a damned and negative way. Still, at least you have being again, you stop drowning, you get your head above water, so that they say, "Look! He's still around." Otherwise, what remains? Superfluity. Nothingness. Doubt that you had ever been alive. There was such a fear of the precipice in the Palace that everyone tried to hold on to His Majesty, still not knowing that the whole court—though slowly and with dignity—was sliding toward the edge of the cliff.

P. M.:

Indeed, my friend, from the moment smoke rose from the Palace a sort of negativism started to flood over us. I have trouble pinning it down, but you could feel negativism all around. You noticed it everywhere on people's faces, faces that seemed diminished and abandoned, without light or energy, in what people did and how they did it. There was negativism in what they said without speaking; in their absent being, as if shrunken, switched off; in their burnt-out existence; in their short-range, small-stuff thinking; in their vegetable-patch, cottage-garden digging; in their weed-grown, overcast look; in the whole atmosphere; in all the immobility—despite the moving around—of the daily grind; in the climate; in the mincing steps. In everything you could feel the negativism flooding over us.

Even though the Emperor went on issuing decrees and striving to get things done, got up early and never rested, all the same the negativism was there, growing all the time, because from the day Germame committed suicide and his brother was captured to be hanged in the main square of the town, a negative system started operating between people and things. People seemed unable to control things; things existed and ceased to exist in their own malicious ways, slipping through people's hands. Everyone felt helpless before the seemingly magic force by which things autonomously appeared and disappeared, and nobody knew how to master or break that force. This feeling of helplessness, of always losing, always falling behind the stronger, drove them deeper into negativism, into numbness, into dejection, into depression, into hiding like partridges. Even conversation deteriorated, losing its vigor and momentum. Conversations started but somehow never seemed to be completed. They always reached an invisible but perceptible point, beyond which silence fell. The silence said, Everything is already known and clear, but clear in an obscure way, known unfathomably, dominating by being beyond helping. Having confirmed this truth by a moment of silence, the conversation changed its direction and moved on to a different subject, a trivial, second-rate, secondhand subject.

The Palace was sinking, and we all felt it, we veterans in the service of His Venerable Majesty, we whom fate had saved from the purge. We could feel the temperature falling, life becoming more and more precisely framed by ritual but more and more cut-and-dried, banal, negative.

**H**e goes on to say that even though the Emperor considered the December upheaval to be over and done with and never returned to the subject, the coup staged by the Neway brothers continued to have destructive consequences for the Palace. As time passed, these consequences grew more powerful rather than weaker, and they changed the life of the Palace and the Empire. Having suffered such a blow, the Palace would never again know true, sweet peace.

Things were gradually changing in town, too. The first mention of disturbances appeared in the secret reports by the police. Fortunately, as my informant says, these were not yet disturbances on a great, revolutionary scale, but rather—at first—tremors, slight oscillations, ambiguous murmurs, whispers, sniggering, a sort of excessive heaviness in people, lying around, drooping, a certain messiness, all expressing some kind of avoidance and refusal. He admits that cleanup operations couldn't start on the basis of these reports. The information was too vague, even comfortingly innocent; it stated that something was hanging in the air, without saying precisely what and where. And without specifics, where was one to send the tanks, and in what direction order the shooting? Usually the reports stated that these murmurs and whispers came from the university—a new one, the only institution of higher learning in the country—in which, from God knows where, there had appeared skeptical, unfriendly individuals, ready to spread harmful and unverified calumnies for the sole purpose of causing new anxieties for the Emperor. He goes on to say that the monarch, in spite of his advanced age, maintained a perspicacity amazing to those around him, and that he understood better than his closest followers that a new era was coming and it was time to pull together, to bring things up to date, to speed up, to catch up. To catch up, and even to overtake. Yes, he insists, even to overtake. He confesses (today one can talk about it) that a part of the Palace was *reluctant to embrace these ambitions, muttering privately that instead of giving in to the temptation of certain novelties and reforms, it would be better to curb the Western inclinations of youth and root out the unreasonable idea that the country should look different, that it should be changed.*

*The Emperor, however, listened to neither the aristocratic grumbling nor the university whispers, believing as he did that all extremes are harmful and unnatural. Demonstrating innate concern and foresight, the Emperor widened the scope of his power and involved himself in new domains, manifesting these new interests by introducing the Hour of Development, the International Hour, and the Army-Police Hour, between four and seven in the afternoon. With the same goals in mind, the Emperor created appropriate ministries and bureaus, branch offices, and commissions, into which he introduced hosts of new people, well behaved, loyal, devoted. A new generation filled the Palace, energetically carving out careers. It was, recalls P.M., the beginning of the 1960's.*

P. M.:

A kind of mania seized this mad and unpredictable world, my friend: a mania for development. Everybody wanted to develop himself! Everyone thought about developing himself, and not simply according to God's law that a man is born, develops, and dies. No, each one wanted to develop himself extraordinarily, dynamically, and powerfully, to develop himself so that everyone would admire, envy, talk, and nod his head. Where it came from, no one knows. Like a herd of sheep, people went crazy with blind greed, and it sufficed that somewhere at the other end of the world someone developed himself; immediately everyone wants to develop himself. Immediately they press, storm, urge that they be developed, too, be raised, that they catch up—and it's enough, my friend, to neglect these voices for you to get mutinies, shouts, rebellions, negativism, frustration, and refusal. Yet our Empire had existed for hundreds, even thousands of years without any noticeable development and all the while its leaders were respected, venerated, worshiped. The Emperors Zera Jakob, Towodros, Johannes all were worshiped. And who would ever have gotten it into his head to press his face to the floor in front of the Emperor and beg to be developed?

However, the world began to change. Our Emperor, innately infallible, noticed and generously agreed with this, seeing the advantages and charms of costly novelty, and since he had always had a weakness for all progress— indeed, he even liked progress—his most honorably benevolent desire for action manifested itself in the unconcealed desire to have a satiated and happy people cry for years after, with full approval, "Hey! Did he ever develop us!" Thus, in the Hour of Development, between four and five in the afternoon, His Highness showed particular vivacity and keenness. He received processions of planners, economists, and financial specialists, talking, asking questions, encouraging, and praising. One was planning, another was building, and so, in a word, development had started. And how. His Indefatigable Majesty would ride out to open a bridge here, a building there, an airport somewhere else, giving these structures his name: the Haile Selassie Bridge in Ogaden, the Haile Selassie Hospital in Harara, the Haile Selassie Hall in the capital, so that whatever was created bore his name. He also laid cornerstones, supervised construction, cut ribbons, took part in the ceremonial starting of a tractor, and everywhere, as I said, he talked, asked questions, encouraged, and praised. A map of the Empire's development hung in the Palace, on which little arrows, stars, and dots lit up, blinking and twinkling so that the dignitaries could gladden their eyes with the sight when His Venerable Majesty pressed a button, although some saw in all this the proof of the Emperor's growing eccentricity. But foreign delegations, whether African or from the wider world, obviously delighted in the map, and upon hearing the Emperor's explanation of the little lights, arrows, and dots, they too talked, asked questions, encouraged, and praised.

And that is how it would have gone on for years, to the joy of His Supreme Highness and his dignitaries, had it not been for our grumbling students, who, since Germame's death, had started to raise their heads more and more, to tell horrendous stories, and to speak unreasonably and insultingly against the Palace. Instead of showing their gratitude for the benefits of enlightenment, those youngsters launched themselves on the turbid and treacherous waters of slander and faction. Alas, my friend, it is a sad truth that, despite His Majesty's having led the Empire onto the path of development, the students reproached the Palace for demagoguery and hypocrisy. How, they said, can one talk of development in the midst of utter poverty? What sort of development is it when the whole nation is being crushed by misery, whole provinces are starving, few can afford a pair of shoes, only a handful of subjects can read and write, anyone who falls seriously ill dies because there are neither hospitals nor physicians, ignorance and illiteracy hold sway everywhere, barbarity, humiliation, trampling underfoot, despotism, exploitation, desperation, and on and on in this tone, dear visitor. Reproaching, calumniating ever more arrogantly, they spoke out against sweetening and dressing things up—taking advantage of His Clement Highness, who only rarely ordered that the mutinous rabble which spilled from the university gates in a larger mass each year be fired upon.

Finally the time came when they brought out their impudent whim of reforming. Development, they said, is impossible without reform. One should give the peasants land, abolish privileges, democratize society, liquidate feudalism, and free the country from dependence on foreigners. From what dependence? I ask. We were independent. We had been an independent country for three thousand years! That's thoughtlessness and running off at the mouth for you. Besides, I ask, how do you reform, how do you reform without everything falling apart? How do you move something without bringing it all tumbling down? But was one of them ever capable of asking himself such a question? To develop and feed everybody simultaneously is also difficult, because where will the money come from? Nobody runs around the world passing out dollars. The Empire produces little and has nothing to export. So how do you fill the treasury? Our Supreme Leader treated that problem with kindly and provident solicitude, considering it a matter of the utmost importance and manifesting his concern incessantly during the International Hour.

T.:

How wonderful international life is! It suffices to recall our visits: airports, greetings, cascades of flowers, embraces, orchestras, every moment polished by protocol, and then limousines, parties, toasts written out and translated, galas and brilliance, praise, confidential conversations, global themes, etiquette, splendor, presents, suites, and finally tiredness, yes, after a whole day tiredness, but how magnificent and relaxing, how refined and honored, how dignified and proper, how—exactly—international! And the next day: sightseeing, stroking children, accepting gifts, excitement, programs, tension—but tension that is pleasant, significant, that frees one for a moment from Palace troubles, displaces

Imperial worries, lets one forget about petitions, coteries, and conspiracies. His Benevolent Highness, however, even when magnificently entertained by his hosts and lit up by the popping flashbulbs, always asked about telegrams with news from the Empire, asked what was with the budget, the army, the police, the students. Even I took part in these worldly splendors, I who was only a member of the sixth decade of the eighth rank of the ninth level.

Please notice, my friend, that our monarch had an exceptional taste for foreign travel. As early as 1924, the first monarch in our history to cross the borders of the Empire, His Gracious Majesty honored the European lands with a visit. There was something of a family inclination to travel, inherited from his father, the late Prince Makonen, who had been sent abroad many times to negotiate with other countries on the orders of the Emperor Menelik. Let me add that His Majesty never lost that inclination, and, even though old age usually makes people inclined to keep close to home, His Indefatigable Majesty traveled more and more as the years went by, inspecting, visiting the most distant countries, losing himself in these peregrinations to such an extent that malicious journalists from the foreign press called him the flying ambassador of his country and asked when he planned to visit his own Empire. This is indeed an appropriate moment, my friend, to pour out all our grievances over the impropriety and maliciousness of the foreign newspapers, which instead of working toward understanding and rapprochement stand ready to commit any baseness and to meddle in internal affairs. And with delight, I may add.

I wonder now why His Venerable Majesty traveled so much in spite of the heavy burden of years that pressed upon his shoulders. It all goes back to the rebellious vanity of the Neway brothers, who forever destroyed the sweet peace of the Empire by pointing out with impious irresponsibility its backwardness and the way it lagged behind everyone else. A few of the journalists picked up such slanders and used them to calumniate His Majesty. Then the students grabbed it and read it, although no one knows how they got their hands on it, because His Most Gracious Majesty forbade the importation of slanders. And so began the pronouncements, criticism, talk of stagnancy and development. His Majesty sensed the spirit of the times, and shortly after the bloody rebellion he ordered complete development. Having done so, he had no choice but to set out on an odyssey from capital to capital, seeking aid, credits, and investment: our Empire was barefoot, skinny, with all its ribs showing. His Majesty demonstrated his superiority over the students by showing them that one can develop without reforming. And how, I hear you asking, is that possible? Well, it is. If you use foreign capital to build the factories, you don't need to reform. So there you are—His Majesty didn't allow reform, yet the factories were going up, they were built. That means development. Just take a ride from downtown toward Debre Zeit. Factories lined up one after the other, modern, automatic!

But now that His Noble Majesty has ended his days in such unseemly abandonment, I can confess that I also had my own thoughts about the Emperor's visits and travels. His Majesty looked more profoundly, more acutely, into things than any of us. He understood that the end was coming and that he was too old to stop the impending avalanche. Older and older, more and more helpless. Tired, exhausted. He needed more relief and freedom from worry. And these visits were a break, a chance for him to rest and catch his breath. At least for a while he didn't have to read the informants' reports, to listen to the roar of crowds and the sound of police gunfire, to look into the faces of toadies and flatterers. He didn't, at least for one day, have to solve the insoluble, repair the irreparable, or cure the incurable. In those foreign countries no one conspired against him, no one was sharpening the knife, no one needed to be hanged. He could go to bed calmly, sure that he would wake up alive. He could sit down with a friendly president and have a relaxing talk, man to man. Yes, my friend, allow me once more to commend the international life. Without it, who could ever bear the burden of governing these days? After all, where is one to look for recognition and understanding if not in the faraway world, in foreign countries, during those intimate conversations with other rulers who will respond to our grief with sympathetic grief, because they have worries and troubles of their own?

But it didn't all seem quite as I'm describing it to you now. Since we've already reached this degree of sincerity, let's admit that in the last years of his reign Our Benefactor had fewer successes and more problems. In spite of every endeavor, his monarchical achievements were not multiplying. And how can anyone justify not having achievements in today's world? Certainly it was possible to invent, to count things twice, to explain, but then troublemakers would immediately stand up and hurl calumnies, and by that time such indecency and perversity had spread that people would rather believe the troublemakers than the Emperor. So His Most Supreme Majesty preferred to set out abroad, to settle disputes, recommend development, lead his brother presidents onto the high road, express concern for the fate of humanity—on the one hand he saved himself from the exhausting troubles at home, and on the other he gained salutary compensation in the form of the splendors and friendly promises of other governments and other courts. You must remember that despite all the hardships of such a long life he never gave up the fight even in the moments of greatest trials and disappointments, and in spite of fatigue and the need for reward he never for a moment considered stepping down from the throne. On the contrary, as adversaries accumulated and the opposition grew, the Emperor observed the Army-Police Hour with exceptional diligence, reinforcing the order and stability necessary to the Empire.


B. H.:

First, I will emphasize that His Majesty, the highest person in the state, was above the law, since he himself constituted the only source of law, and he was not subject to any of its norms and regulations. He was supreme in everything, in all that had been created by God or man, and therefore also he was supreme commander of the army and the police. He had to exercise particular care and discrimination in his supervision of the two institutions, especially since the December events proved that shameful disorder, abusive opinions, and even sacrilegious treason had taken root among the ranks of the Imperial Guard and the police. Fortunately, the army generals had shown their loyalty in that unexpected hour of trial and made possible a dignified though painful return of the Emperor to his Palace. But having saved his throne, they now started to importune the Supreme Benefactor, asking to be paid for that service. Such was the down-to-earth attitude prevalent in the army that they computed their loyalty in money terms and even expected His Benevolent Highness, of his own initiative, to stuff their pockets full, oblivious to the fact that privileges corrupt and corruption stains the honor of the uniform. This impudence and aggressiveness spread from the army generals to the head police officers, who also wanted to be corrupted, to be showered with privileges, to have their pockets stuffed. All because, having observed the progressive weakening of the Palace, they cleverly deduced that our monarch was going to need them often and that in the end they constituted the surest, and in critical moments the only, prop of sovereign power.

And so His Unrivaled Highness had to introduce the Army-Police Hour, during which he bestowed abundant favors on the highest-ranking officers and expressed his concern about the state of those institutions that secured the internal order and stability for which the people thanked heaven. These generals, with His Gracious Majesty's help, arranged such a good life for themselves that in our Empire, which contained thirty million farmers and only a hundred thousand soldiers and police, agriculture received one percent of the national budget and the army and police forty percent. This provided the students with subject matter for their cracker-barrel philosophizing and wisecracks. But were they right? Did not His Majesty create the first regular army in our history, an army paid out of the Imperial cashbox? Before that our armies always assembled from a levy en masse. When summoned, soldiers set out for the battle-field from all corners of the Empire, stealing whatever they could along the way, plundering the villages in their path, butchering peasants and cattle. After such incidents—and they occurred endlessly—the monarchy was a shambles and couldn't get back on its feet for a long time. So His Venerable Highness punished robbery, forbade the levy en masse, and entrusted to the British the task of forming a regular army, which they did as soon as the Italians had been pushed out.

His Distinguished Majesty had a great fondness for his army. He willingly reviewed parades, and he liked to put on his Emperor-marshall's uniform, to which rows of colorful decorations and medals added splendor. However, his Imperial dignity would not allow him to probe too deeply into the details of barracks life or to investigate the condition of the simple soldier and lower officer, and the Palace machine for deciphering military codes must have been out of order much of the time, because it came out later that the Emperor did not even know what was going on behind army walls, a state of affairs that unfortunately caught up in a disastrous way with the affairs of the Empire.

P. M.:

. . . and as a consequence of Our Benefactor's concern to develop the forces of order and thanks to his great generosity in that area, the number of policemen multiplied during the last years of his reign, and ears appeared everywhere, sticking up out of the ground, glued to the walls, flying through the air, hanging on doorknobs, hiding in offices, lurking in crowds, standing in doorways, jostling in the marketplace. To protect themselves from the plague of informers, people learned—without anyone knowing how or where, or when, without schools, without courses, without records or dictionaries—another language, mastered it, and became so fluent in it that we simple and uneducated folk suddenly became a bilingual nation. It was extremely helpful; it even saved lives and preserved the peace and allowed people to exist. Each of the two languages had a different vocabulary, a different set of meanings, even a different grammar, and yet everyone overcame these difficulties in time and learned to express himself in the proper language. One tongue served for external speech, the other for internal. The first was sweet and the second bitter, the first polished and the second coarse, one allowed to come to the surface and the other kept out of sight. And everybody made his own choice, according to conditions and circumstances, whether to expose his tongue or to hide it, to uncover it or to keep it under wraps.

M.:

And just think, my friend, amid all this flowering development, amid the success and well-being proclaimed by our
monarch, suddenly an uprising breaks out. A thunderbolt
from a clear blue sky! In the Palace—astonishment, surprise,
running back and forth, bustle, His August Majesty asking,
"Where did it come from?" And how can we, humble servants, answer him? Accidents happen to people, don't they?
So they can also happen to an Empire, and in 1968 this is
what happened to us: in Gojam Province the peasants
jumped on their rulers' throats. All the notables found it
inconceivable, because we had a docile, resigned, God-fearing people not at all inclined to rebellion, and here, as I said,
suddenly, for no reason whatever—mutiny! To us humility
is uppermost and even His Majesty, as a young lad, kissed
his father's shoes. When the elders were eating, children had
to stand with their faces to the wall to avoid any ungodly
temptation of considering themselves equal to their parents.
I mention this, dear friend, to help you understand that if
the peasants in such a country go on a rampage, they must
have an extraordinary reason.

Let us admit here that the reason was a certain clumsy
overzealousness of the Finance Ministry. These were the
years of enforced development, which brought us so many
worries. Why worries? Because in advocating progress His
Highness whetted the appetites and whims of his subjects.
Eager to be thus encouraged, the people thought that development meant pleasure and treats, and they kept demanding provender and progress, delicacies in excess. But
the greatest troubles sprang from the progress in enlightenment, because the multiplying numbers of school graduates
had to be placed in offices, thereby causing the ascendancy
of the bureaucracy, which waxed enormous as His Majesty's
cashbox waned. And how can you make clerks tighten their

belts when they are the most stable and loyal element? A clerk will slander you behind your back, grumble secretly, but when called to order he will shut up and, if need be, turn out to support you. You can't put the courtiers on hard rations, either, because they are the Palace family. Nor the officers—they secure peaceful development. And so during the Hour of the Cashbox a multitude of people showed up, and the purse dwindled away because every day His Benevolent Majesty had to pay more for loyalty.

Since the cost of loyalty was going up, there was an urgent need to increase income, and that's why the Finance Ministry ordered the peasants to pay higher taxes. Today I am free to say that it was His Unrivaled Majesty's decision, but because the Emperor, as a gracious benefactor, could not issue vexatious or plaguing decrees, any proclamation that put a new burden on the shoulders of the people was issued in the name of some ministry. If the people could not shoulder that burden and started a rebellion, His Majesty scolded the ministry and replaced the minister— although he never did so immediately, to avoid creating the humiliating impression that the monarch allows the unbridled mob to put his Palace in order. On the contrary, when he saw the need to demonstrate monarchical supremacy he would raise the most disliked officials to higher positions, as if to say, "Get an eyeload of who's really in charge here, of who makes the impossible possible!" His Noble Majesty asserted his force and authority by benevolently needling his subjects.

Yet now, my gracious sir, reports are coming in from Gojam Province that the peasants are brawling, rebelling, bashing in the skulls of tax collectors, hanging policemen, running dignitaries out of town, burning down estates, uprooting crops. The governor reports that rebels are storming the offices and that whenever they get their hands on the

Emperor's people they vilify them, torture them, and quarter them. Obviously, the longer the submissiveness, the silence, and the shouldering of burdens, the greater the hostility and cruelty. And in the capital the students defend the rebels, praising them, pointing a finger at the court, hurling insults. Fortunately that province is so situated that it could be cut off, surrounded by the army, shot up, and bled into submission. But until that was accomplished you could sense a great fear in the Palace, because you never can tell how far boiling water will spill. That is why His Providential Majesty, seeing the Empire wobbling, first sent the strike force to Gojam to take the peasants' heads off, then, confronting the incomprehensible resistance put up by the rebels, ordered the new taxes repealed and scolded the ministry for its overzealousness.

His August Majesty chided the bureaucrats for failing to understand a simple principle: the principle of the second bag. Because the people never revolt just because they have to carry a heavy load, or because of exploitation. They don't know life without exploitation, they don't even know that such a life exists. How can they desire what they cannot imagine? The people will revolt only when, in a single movement, someone tries to throw a second burden, a second heavy bag, onto their backs. The peasant will fall face down into the mud—and then spring up and grab an ax. He'll grab an ax, my gracious sir, not because he simply can't sustain this new burden—he could carry it—he will rise because he feels that, in throwing the second burden onto his back suddenly and stealthily, you have tried to cheat him, you have treated him like an unthinking animal, you have trampled what remains of his already strangled dignity, taken him for an idiot who doesn't see, feel, or understand. A man doesn't seize an ax in defense of his wallet, but in defense of his dignity, and that, dear sir, is why

His Majesty scolded the clerks. For their own convenience and vanity, instead of adding the burden bit by bit, in little bags, they tried to heave a whole big sack on at once.

So, in order to ensure future peace for the Empire, His Majesty immediately set the clerks to work sewing little bags. He had them add to the burden in little bags, taking a break between one bag and the next and keenly watching the expressions on the faces of the burdened, judging whether or not they can stand a little more, whether one should add a wee bit or let them breathe for a while. In that, my dear friend, lay the whole art: in not doing it all at once thickly and blindly, but rather carefully, kindly, reading the faces to know when to add, when to tighten the screw and when to loosen it. Thus, after some time had passed and the blood had soaked into the ground and the wind had blown away the smoke, the clerks started adding taxes again, but this time they dosed it and bagged it gently, carefully, and the peasants bore it all and took no offense.

Z. S.-K.:

A year after the Gojam uprising—which by showing the furious and unrelenting face of the people stirred the Palace and threw a fright into the dignitaries (and not only them: we servants also started getting the creeps)—a singular misfortune happened to me: my son Hailu, a university student in those depressing years, began to think. That's right, he began to think, and I must explain to you, my friend, that in those days thinking was a painful inconvenience and a troubling deformity. His Unexcelled Majesty, in his incessant care for the good and comfort of his subjects, never spared any efforts to protect them from this inconvenience and deformity. Why should they waste the time that ought to be devoted to the cause of development, why should they disturb their internal peace and stuff their heads with all sorts of disloyal ideas? Nothing decent or comforting could result if someone decided to think restlessly and provocatively or mingle with those who were thinking. And yet my harebrained son committed exactly that indiscretion. My wife was the first to notice it. Her maternal instinct told her that dark clouds were gathering over our home, and she said to me one day, "Hailu must have started to think. You can see that he's sad." That's how it was then. Those who surveyed the Empire and pondered their surroundings walked sadly and lost in thought, their eyes full of troubled pensiveness, as if they had a presentiment of something vague and unspeakable. Most often one saw such faces among students, who, let me add, were causing His Majesty a lot of grief. It truly amazes me that the police never caught the scent, the connection between thinking and mood. Had they made that discovery in time they could easily have neutralized these thinkers, who by their snorting and malicious reluctance to show satisfaction brought so many troubles and afflictions on His Venerable Majesty's head.

The Emperor, however, showing more perspicacity than his police, understood that sadness can drive one to thinking, disappointment, waffling, and shuffling, and so he ordered distractions, merriment, festivities, and masquerades for the whole Empire. His Noble Majesty himself had the Palace illuminated, threw banquets for the poor, and incited people to gaiety. When they had guzzled and gamboled, they gave praise to their King. This went on for years, and the distractions so filled people's heads, so corked them up, that they could talk of nothing but having fun. Our feet are bare, but we're debonair, hey ho! Only the thinkers, who saw everything getting gray, shrunken, mud-splashed, and moldy, skipped the jokes and the merriment. They became a nuisance. The unthinking ones were wiser; they didn't let themselves get taken in, and when the students started holding rallies and talking, the nonthinkers stuffed their ears and made themselves scarce. What's the use of knowing, when it's better not to know? Why do it the hard way, when it can be easy? Why talk, if you're better off keeping your mouth shut? Why get mixed up in the affairs of the Empire, when there's so much to do closer to home, when there's shopping to be done?

Well, my friend, seeing what a dangerous course my son was sailing, I tried to dissuade him, to encourage him to participate in amusements, to send him on excursions. I would even have preferred that he devote himself to nightlife rather than to those damned demonstrations and conspiracies. Just imagine my pain, my distress: the father in the Palace, the son in the anti-Palace. In the streets I'm protected by the police from my own son, who demonstrates and throws rocks. I told him over and over again, "Why don't you give up thinking? It doesn't get you anywhere. Forget it. Fool around instead. Look at other people, those who listen to the wise—how cheerfully they walk around, laugh. No clouds on their foreheads. They devote themselves to the good life, and if they worry about anything it's about how to fill their pockets, and to such concerns and solicitations His Majesty is always kindly inclined, always thinking of how to make things smooth and cozy." "And how," asks Hailu, "can there be a contradiction between a person who thinks and a wise person? If a person doesn't think, he's a fool." "Not at all," I say. "Wise he still is—it's just that he has directed his thoughts to a safe, sheltered place, and not between rumbling, crushing millstones." But it was too late. Hailu was already living in a different world; by then the university, located not far from the Palace, had turned itself into a real anti-Palace where only the brave set foot, and the space between the court and the university increasingly resembled a battlefield on which the fate of the Empire was being decided.

*His thoughts return to the December events, when the commander of the Imperial Guard, Mengistu Neway, came to the university to show the students the dry bread with which the rebels had fed those closest to the Emperor. This event was a shock that the students never forgot. One of Haile Selassie's closest and most trusted officers represented the Emperor—a divine being, with supernatural attributes —as a man who tolerated corruption in the Palace, defended a backward system, and accepted the misery of millions of his subjects. That day the fight began, and the university never again knew peace. The tumultuous conflict between the Palace and the university, lasting almost fourteen years, engulfed scores of victims and ended only with the overthrow of the Emperor.*

*In those years there existed two images of Haile Selassie. One, known to international opinion, presented the Emperor as a rather exotic, gallant monarch, distinguished by indefatigable energy, a sharp mind, and profound sensitivity, a man who made a stand against Mussolini, recovered his Empire and his throne, and had ambitions of developing his country and playing an important role in the world. The other image, formed gradually by a critical and initially small segment of Ethiopian opinion, showed the monarch as a ruler committed to defending his power at any cost, a man who was above all a great demagogue and a theatrical paternalist who used words and gestures to mask the corruption and servility of a ruling elite that he had created and coddled. And, as often happens, both these images were correct. Haile Selassie had a complex personality, and to some he was full of charm while among others he provoked hatred. Some adored him, while others cursed him. He ruled a country that knew only the cruelest methods of fighting for power (or of keeping it), in which free elections were replaced by poison and the dagger, discussions by shooting and the gallows. He was a product of this tradition, and he himself fell back upon it. Yet at the same time he understood that there was an impossibility in it, that it was out of touch with the new world. But he could not change the system that kept him in power, and for him power came first. Hence the flights into demagoguery, into ceremony, into speeches about development—all so very empty in this country of oppressive misery and ignorance. He was a most amiable personage, a shrewd politician, a tragic father, a pathological miser. He condemned innocence to death and pardoned guilt. Whims of power, labyrinths of Palace politics, ambiguity, darkness that no one could penetrate.*

Z. S.-K.:

Immediately after the Gojam uprising, Prince Kassa wanted to gather loyal students and stage a demonstration in support of the Emperor. Everything was prepared, portraits and banners, when His Noble Majesty found out about it and rebuked the prince sharply. All demonstrations were out of the question. They begin with support and end up with invective. They start with cheering, and end with shooting. Once more, my friend, you see here the awe-inspiring prescience of His Supreme Highness. In the general confusion they didn't manage to call off the demonstration. When the march of the supporters, composed of policemen disguised as students, started, a great and rebellious mass of real students quickly joined it, this ominous rabble started rolling toward the Palace, and there was no other solution but to bring out the army to enforce the restoration of order. In this unfortunate confrontation, which ended in bloodshed, the leader of the students, Tilahum Gizaw, perished. What an irony it was that several of the policemen died, too, and yet were they not completely innocent? This, I remember, was at the end of 1969.

The next day was awful for me. Hailu and all his friends went to the funeral, and such a crowd gathered at the coffin that it turned into a new demonstration. The continuous ferment and unrest in the capital could no longer be tolerated, so His Distinguished Majesty sent in armored personnel carriers and commanded that order be restored in no uncertain terms. As a result more than twenty students perished and countless others were wounded and arrested. His Highness ordered that the university be closed for a year, thus saving the lives of many young people. Because if they had been studying, demonstrating, and storming the Palace, the Emperor would have had to respond again by clubbing, shooting, and spilling blood.

# THE COLLAPSE

It is an amazing thing, the extraordinary feeling of security in which all those tenants of the highest and middle stories of the social edifice were living when the revolution broke out. In all naïveté of spirit they were discoursing on the people's virtues, greatness, and loyalty, of their innocent joys, when the year '93 was hanging over them: a comic and terrible sight.

(de Tocqueville, *The Ancien Régime and the Revolution*)

And something else besides, something invisible, a directing spirit of perdition that dwelt within.

(Conrad, *Lord Jim*)

On the other hand, the courtiers of Justinian who stayed at his side in the palace until the late hours had the impression that, instead of him, they saw a strange phantom. One of them claimed that the Emperor would spring suddenly from the throne and start pacing up and down the chamber (indeed, he could no longer stay in one place); all of a sudden Justinian's head would disappear, but the body would go on pacing. The courtier, thinking his eyesight had betrayed him, stood for a long while helpless and confused. Afterward, however, when the head returned to its place on the torso, he found himself amazed to see what had not been there a moment ago.

(Procopius, *The Secret History*)

Next I ask myself the question, Where is it all now? Smoke, ashes, fable. Or perhaps it is no longer even a fable.

(Marcus Aurelius, *Meditations*)

Nobody's candle keeps burning until the very dawn.

(Ivo Andrić, *The Consuls of Their Imperial Highnesses*)

M. S.:

For many years I served as mortarman to His Most Extraordinary Highness. I used to set up the mortar near the place where the kindly monarch gave feasts for the poor, who craved food. As the banquet was ending, I would fire a series of projectiles. When they burst, these projectiles released a colored cloud that slowly floated to the ground— colored handkerchiefs bearing the likeness of the Emperor. The people crowded, pushing each other, stretching out their hands, everyone wanting to return home with a picture of His Highness that had miraculously dropped from the sky.


A. A.:

Nobody, but nobody, my friend, had any foreboding that the end was drawing near. Or rather, one did sense something, something haunting, but so vague, so indistinct, that it was not like a presentiment of the extraordinary. For a long time there had been a valet de chambre who floated around the Palace, turning off lights here and there. But one's eyes got used to the dimness, and there followed a comfortable inner resignation to the fact that everything had to be turned off, extinguished, obscured. What's more, shameful disorder crept into the Empire, disorder that caused annoyance to the whole Palace, but most of all to our Minister of Information, Mr. Tesfaye Gebre-Egzy, later shot by the rebels who rule today.

This is how it began. In 1973, in the summer, a certain Jonathan Dimbleby, a journalist from London television, came to our country. He had visited the Empire before and made commendable films about His Supreme Majesty, and so it occurred to no one that such a journalist, who had earlier praised, would dare to criticize later. But such is obviously the dastardly nature of people without dignity or faith. Anyway, this time, instead of showing how His Highness attends to development and cares for the prosperity of the little ones, Dimbleby went up north, from where he supposedly returned perturbed and shaken. Right away he left for England. A month hadn't passed when a report came from our embassy there that Mr. Dimbleby had shown a film entitled *Ethiopia: The Unknown Famine* on London TV, in which this unprincipled calumniator pulled the demagogic trick of showing thousands of people dying of hunger, and next to that His Venerable Highness feasting with dignitaries. Then he showed roads on which scores of poor, famished skeletons were lying, and immediately afterward our airplanes bringing champagne and caviar from Europe. Here, whole fields of dying scrags; there, His Highness serving meat to his dogs from a silver platter. This, then that: splendor—misery, riches—despair, corruption—death. In addition, Mr. Dimbleby announced that hunger had already caused the death of a hundred thousand people, perhaps even two hundred thousand, and that twice that number might share their fate in the very near future. The report from the embassy said that after the film was shown, a great scandal broke out in London. There were appeals to Parliament, the newspapers raised alarms, His Royal Highness was condemned.

Here you can see, my friend, the irresponsibility of the foreign press, which like Mr. Dimbleby praised our monarch for years and then suddenly, without any rhyme or reason, condemned him. Why? Why such treason and immorality? The embassy reports that a whole airplaneload of European journalists is taking off from London, to come see death from hunger, to know our reality, and to determine where the money goes that their governments have given to His August Majesty for development, catching up, and surpassing. Bluntly speaking, interference in the internal affairs of the Empire! In the Palace, commotion and indignation, but His Most Singular Highness counsels calm and discretion. Now we await the highest decisions. Right away voices sound for recalling the ambassador, who sent such unpleasant and alarming reports and brought so much unrest into the Palace. However, the Minister of Foreign Affairs argues that such a recall will put fear into the remaining ambassadors and make them stop reporting, and yet His Venerable Highness needs to know what is said about him in various parts of the world. Next the members of the Crown Council speak up, demanding that the airplane carrying the journalists be turned back and that none of the blasphemous rabble be let into the Empire. But how, asks the Minister of Information, can we not let them in? They'll raise hell and condemn His Gracious Majesty more than ever.

After much deliberation they decide to offer His Benevolent Highness the following solution: let them in, but deny the hunger. Keep them in Addis Ababa, show them the development, and let them write only what can be read in our newspapers. And I'll go so far, my friend, as to say that we had a loyal press—yes, loyal in an exemplary way. To tell the truth, there wasn't much of it, because for over thirty million subjects twenty-five thousand copies were printed daily, but His Highness worked on the assumption that even the most loyal press should not be given in abundance, because that might create a habit of reading, and from there it is only a single step to the habit of thinking, and it is well known what inconveniences, vexations, troubles, and worries thinking causes. For even what is written loyally can be read disloyally. Someone will start to read a loyal text, then he will want a disloyal one, and so he will follow the road that leads him away from the throne, away from development, and straight toward the malcontents. No, no, His Majesty could not allow such demoralization to happen, such straying, and that's why in general he wasn't an enthusiast of excessive reading.

Soon afterward we suffered a real invasion of foreign correspondents. A press conference took place immediately after their arrival. "What," they ask, "does the problem of death from hunger, which decimates the population, look like?" "I know nothing of any such matter," answers the Minister of Information, and I must tell you, friend, that he wasn't far from the truth. First of all, death from hunger had existed in our Empire for hundreds of years, an everyday, natural thing, and it never occurred to anyone to make any noise about it. Drought would come and the earth would dry up, the cattle would drop dead, the peasants would starve. Ordinary, in accordance with the laws of nature and the eternal order of things. Since this was eternal and normal, none of the dignitaries would dare to bother His Most Exalted Highness with the news that in such and such a province a given person had died of hunger. Of course, His Benevolent Highness visited the provinces himself, but it was not his custom to stop in poor regions where there was hunger, and anyway how much can one see during official visits? Palace people didn't spend much time in the provinces either, because it was enough for a man to leave the Palace and they would gossip about him, report on him, so that when he came back he would find that his enemies had moved him closer to the street. So how were we to know that there was unusual hunger up north?

"Can we," ask the correspondents, "go north?" "No, you can't," explains the minister, "because the roads are full of bandits." Again, I must remark, he wasn't far from the truth, because increased incidents of armed disloyalty near highways all over the Empire had been much reported of late. And then the minister took them for an excursion around the capital, showing them factories and praising the development. But with that gang, forget it! They don't want development, they demand hunger and that's all there is to it. "Well," says the minister, "you won't get hunger. How can there be hunger if there is development?"

But here, my friend, there was a new development. Our rebellious students sent their delegates north, and they came back with photographs and terrible stories about how the nation is dying—and all this they passed along to the correspondents on the sly. So a scandal broke out. You could no longer say that there was no hunger. And once more the correspondents attack, they wave the pictures, they ask what the government has done about hunger. "His Most Supreme Majesty," the minister answers, "has attached the utmost importance to this matter." "But specifically! Specifically what?" this devilish rabble cries disrespectfully. "His Majesty," the minister says calmly, "will announce in due time his intended royal decisions, assignments, and directions, because it is not fitting for ministers to do so." Finally the correspondents flew away, without seeing hunger close up. And this whole affair, conducted so smoothly and in such a dignified manner, the minister considered a success and our press called a victory, which was fine, but we feared that if the minister were to disappear tomorrow we would have nothing but sorrow. And that was exactly what happened later, when the rebels put him against the wall.

Consider also, my dear friend, that—between you and me —it is not bad for national order and a sense of national humility that the subjects be rendered skinnier, thinned down a bit. Our religion ordains a strict fast for half of all the days in the year, and our commandments say that whoever breaks the fast commits a deadly sin and begins to stink all over of hellish sulfur. During a fast day one cannot eat more than once, and then only a piece of unleavened bread with spices for seasoning. Why did our fathers impose such strict rules on us, recommending that mortification of the flesh be practiced unceasingly? It is because man is by nature a bad creature who takes damning pleasure out of giving in to temptations, especially the temptations of disobedience, possessiveness, and licentiousness. Two lusts breed in the soul of man: the lust for aggression, and the lust for telling lies. If one will not allow himself to wrong others, he will wrong himself. If he doesn't come across anyone to lie to, he will lie to himself in his own thoughts. Sweet to man is the bread of untruths, says the Book of Proverbs, and then with sand his mouth is filled up.

How, then, is one to confront this threatening creature that man seems to be, that we all are? How to tame him and daunt him? How to know that beast, how to master it? There is only one way, my friend: by weakening him. Yes, by depriving him of his vitality, because without it he will be incapable of wrong. And to weaken is exactly what fasting does. Such is our Amharic philosophy, and this is what our fathers teach us. Experience confirms it. A man starved all his life will never rebel. Up north there was no rebellion. No one raised his voice or his hand there. But just let the subject start to eat his fill and then try to take the bowl away, and immediately he rises in rebellion. The usefulness of going hungry is that a hungry man thinks only of bread. He's all wrapped up in the thought of food. He loses the remains of his vitality in that thought, and he no longer has either the desire or the will to seek pleasure through the temptation of disobedience. Just think: Who destroyed our Empire? Who reduced it to ruin? Neither those who had too much, nor those who had nothing, but those who had a bit. Yes, one should always beware of those who have a bit, because they are the worst, they are the greediest, it is they who push upward.

Z. S.-K.:

Great discontent, even condemnation and indignation, reigned in the Palace because of the disloyalty of European governments, which allowed Mr. Dimbleby and his ilk to raise such a din on the subject of starvation. Some of the dignitaries wanted to keep on denying, but that was no longer possible since the minister himself had told the correspondents that His Most Sovereign Highness attached the greatest importance to hunger. So we eagerly entered on the new road and asked the foreign benefactors for help. We ourselves do not have, so let others give what they can. Not much time had passed before good news came. Airplanes loaded with wheat landed, ships full of flour and sugar sailed in. Physicians and missionaries came, people from philanthropic organizations, students from foreign colleges, and also correspondents disguised as male nurses. The whole crowd marched north to the provinces of Tigre and Welo, and also east to Ogaden, where, they say, whole tribes had perished of hunger.

International traffic in the Empire! I'll say right off that there wasn't much joy about it in the Palace. It's never good to let so many foreigners in, since they are amazed at everything and they criticize everything. You can imagine, Mr. Richard, that our notables were not disappointed in their fears. When these missionaries, physicians, and so-called nurses reached the north, they saw a thing most amazing to them, namely, thousands dying of hunger right next door to markets and stores full of food. There is food, they say, only there was a bad harvest and the peasants had to give it all to the landowners and that's why they've got nothing left and the speculators took advantage and raised the prices so high that hardly anyone could buy wheat and that's where the misery comes from. An unpleasant affair, Mr. Richard, since it was our notables who were the speculators, and how can one call by such a name the official representatives of His Well-Beloved Highness? Official and speculator? No, no, one can't say that at all!

That's why, when the shouts of these missionaries and nurses reached the capital, voices were immediately raised demanding that these benefactors and philosophers be expelled from the Empire. But how, say the others, can we expel? We cannot possibly stop the action against hunger, since His Benevolent Majesty has attached the greatest importance to it! So once again no one knows what to do: expel—wrong; keep—also wrong. A sort of vacillation and vagueness develops, when suddenly a new thunderbolt strikes. Now the nurses and missionaries are raising hell, saying that the transports of flour and sugar are not reaching those who are starving. Something is happening, say the benefactors, so that the aid is disappearing along the way, and somebody should find out where it is getting lost. They start to poke about, to interfere, to nose around. Once more it turns out that the speculators are packing whole shipments into their warehouses, jacking up the prices, and stuffing their pockets. How this was discovered, it is difficult to say. There must have been some leaks. Things were set up so that the Empire would accept the aid and take care of distribution itself, and no one was to try to figure out where the flour and sugar were going—that would be interference. Now our students get ready for action. They shout in the streets, denounce the corrupt, mount cries for indictments. "Shame!" they scream, proclaiming the death of the Empire. The police club them, arrest them. Upheaval, seething, commotion.

During this period, Mr. Richard, my son Hailu was a rare guest in our home. The university was already engaged in open war with the Palace. This time it started with a completely trivial affair, with a small, insignificant event, so small that nobody would have noticed, nobody would have thought—and yet obviously there come such moments when the smallest event, just a trifle, any bit of nonsense, will provoke a revolution and unleash a war. That is why our police commander, General Yilma Shibeshi, was right when he ordered that no stone be left unturned, that there be no lying around but rather diligent searching with a fine-tooth comb, and that the principle never be forgotten that if a seed starts to sprout, immediately, without waiting for it to grow into something, the plant should be cut down. The general himself looked, and yet, obviously, he found nothing. The trivial event that set things off was a fashion show at the university, organized by the American Peace Corps even though all gatherings and meetings were forbidden. But His Distinguished Majesty could not forbid the Americans a show, could he? And so the students took advantage of this cheerful and carefree event to gather in an enormous crowd and set off for the Palace. And from that moment on they never again let themselves be driven back to their homes. They held meetings, they stormed implacably and vehemently, they did not yield again. And General Shibeshi was tearing his hair out, because not even to him had it occurred that a revolution could start at a fashion show.

But that is exactly how it looked to us. "Father," says Hailu, "this is the beginning of the end for all of you. We cannot live like this any longer. This death up north and the lies of the court have covered us with shame. The country is drowning in corruption, people are dying of hunger, ignorance, and barbarity everywhere. We feel ashamed of this country. And yet we have no other country, we have to dig it out of the mud ourselves. Your Palace has compromised us before the world, and such a Palace can no longer exist. We know that there is unrest in the army and unrest in the city, and now we cannot back down." Yes, Mr. Richard, among these noble but very irresponsible people one was struck by the deep feelings of shame about the state of the fatherland. For them there existed only the twentieth century, or perhaps even this twenty-first century everyone is waiting for, in which blessed justice will reign. Nothing else suited them anymore, everything else irritated them. They didn't see what they wanted to see, and so, apparently, they decided to arrange the world so that they would be able to look at it with contentment. Oh well, Mr. Richard, young people, very young people!

T. L.:

Amid all the people starving, missionaries and nurses clamoring, students rioting, and police cracking heads, His Serene Majesty went to Eritrea, where he was received by his grandson, Fleet Commander Eskinder Desta, with whom he intended to make an official cruise on the flagship *Ethiopia*. They could only manage to start one engine, however, and the cruise had to be called off. His Highness then moved on to the French ship *Protet*, where he was received on board for dinner by Hiele, the well-known admiral from Marseille. The next day, in the port of Massawa, His Most Ineffable Highness raised himself for the occasion to the rank of Grand Admiral of the Imperial Fleet, and made seven cadets officers, thereby increasing our naval power. Also he summoned the wretched notables from the north who had been accused by the missionaries and nurses of speculation and stealing from the starving, and he conferred high distinctions on them to prove that they were innocent and to curb the foreign gossip and slander.

Everything seemed to be moving along well, developing favorably and successfully and most loyally; the Empire was growing and even, as His Supreme Highness stressed, blossoming—when suddenly reports came in that those overseas benefactors who had taken upon themselves the trouble of feeding our ever-insatiable people had rebelled and were suspending shipments because our Finance Minister, Mr. Yelma Deresa, wanting to enrich the Imperial treasury, had ordered the benefactors to pay high customs fees on the aid. "You want to help?" the minister asked. "Please do, but you must pay." And they said, "What do you mean, pay? We give help! And we're supposed to pay?" "Yes," says the minister, "those are the regulations. Do you want to help in such a way that our Empire gains nothing by it?" And here, together with the minister, our press raises its voice to denounce the rebellious benefactors, saying that by suspending aid they condemn our nation to the cruelties of poverty and starvation. They oppose the Emperor and interfere in internal affairs. It was rumored, my friend, that half a million people had died of hunger, which our newspapers blamed on these shameful, infamous missionaries and nurses. Mr. Gebre-Egzy called the strategy of accusing these altruists of waste and starving the nation a success, and the newspapers unanimously confirmed his opinion.

At that very moment, amid all the publicity and writing about the new success, His Venerable Highness, having left the hospitable decks of the French vessel, returned to the capital to be greeted as humbly and thankfully as ever. And yet, if I may now say so, in this humility one sensed a certain vagueness, a sort of obscure duplicity, a sort of, well, humble lack of humility, and the thankfulness was not demonstrated eagerly, but rather reticently and sulkily. True, they did give thanks, but how passive it was, how sluggish, how ungrateful a thanksgiving! This time, as always, people fell on their faces when the procession drove by, but how could it ever compare to the old falling? In the old days, my friend, it used to be real falling—sinking to the point of losing oneself, falling into dust, into ashes, into a shivering, quivering fit on the ground, hands reaching out and beseeching mercy. And now? Sure, they fell, but it was such an unanimated falling, so sleepy, as if imposed on them, as if done only for the sake of peace—slow, lazy, simply negative. Yes, they were falling negatively, awkwardly, grimacing. It seemed to me that, even as their bodies fell, deep down they were standing. They seemed to be lying face to the ground, but in their thoughts they were sitting, acting humbly with hearts that grumbled. Nobody in the procession noticed this, however—and even if anyone had observed a certain indolence and sluggishness, he wouldn't have said anything about it, because any expression of doubt was received badly by the Palace. The nobles had little time, after all, and if one person expressed doubt, everybody else had to put aside what they were doing and dispel these doubts, remove them completely, in fact, and cheer up the doubtful one.

On his return to the Palace, His Prudent Highness accepted a denunciation from the Minister of Commerce, Ketema Yfru, who accused the Finance Minister of interrupting aid to the hungry by imposing the high customs fees. However, His Benevolent Majesty did not reprimand Mr. Yelma Deresa with a single harsh word; on the contrary, manifest satisfaction shone on the royal countenance. His Sovereign Majesty had accepted the aid unwillingly because of all the publicity that accompanied it; all the sighing and headshaking over those who were wasting away spoiled the flourishing and imposing image of the Empire, which, after all, was marching along the road of undisturbed development, catching up and even surpassing. From that moment no aid or contributions were needed. For the starvelings it had to suffice that His Munificent Highness personally attached the greatest importance to their fate, which was a very special kind of attachment, of an order higher than the highest. It provided the subjects with a soothing and uplifting hope that whenever there appeared in their lives an oppressive mischance, some tormenting difficulty, His Most Unrivaled Highness would hearten them—by attaching the greatest importance to that mischance or difficulty.

D.:

The last year! Yes, but who then could have foreseen that 1974 would be our last year? Well, yes, one did feel a sort of vagueness, a melancholy chaotic ineptness, a certain negativity, something heavy in the air, nervousness and tension, flabbiness, now dawning, now growing dark, but how did we go so quickly straight into the abyss? That's it? No more? You can look, but no more Palace. You seek, but you do not find. You ask, but no one can answer. And it began . . . well, that's the point. It began so many times, and yet it never ended. There were so many beginnings but no definite ending, and because of this unending beginning, through so many unfinished starts, your soul grew accustomed to it all. There arose a conviction that we would always wriggle out of it, lift ourselves up again, that we would hold on to whatever we had a grip on and hang on through the worst.

But this growing accustomed to things ended in a mistake. In January 1974 General Beleta Abebe stopped over in the Gode barracks on his way to an inspection in Ogaden. The next day an incredible report came to the Palace: the general has been arrested by the soldiers, who are forcing him to eat what they eat. Food so obviously rotten that some fear the general will fall ill and die. The Emperor sends in the airborne unit of his Guard, which liberates the general and takes him to the hospital. Now, sir, a scandal should break out because His Revered Majesty devoted all his attention to the army during the Army-Police Hour, continually raising its pay and increasing its budget, and suddenly it comes out that the generals have been putting all the raises into their pockets and making great fortunes. However, the Emperor did not scold any of the generals, and he ordered that the soldiers from Gode be dispersed.

After this unpleasant incident, worthy of oblivion, indicating a certain insubordination in the army—we had the biggest army in black Africa, the object of His Majesty's unabashed pride—calm set in. Only for a while, though, because a month later a new report comes in to the Palace, also unheard of! In the southern province of Sidamo, in the Negele garrison, the soldiers start a rebellion and arrest their superiors. It began because the soldiers' wells in this dinky tropical nowhere dried up and their superiors forbade the soldiers to drink from the officers' well. The soldiers lost their senses because of thirst and started a rebellion. The airborne unit of the Imperial Guard should have been sent in to pacify them, but remember, my dear sir, that this was the terrible and unimaginable month of February, when in the capital itself events of such a sudden and revolutionary nature were occurring that everyone forgot about the unruly soldiers in distant Negele, who, having seized the officers' well, were now drinking their fill. It so happened that just then it was necessary to begin stamping out a mutiny that had erupted in the very neighborhood of the Palace.

How very surprising was the cause of this violent unrest that took over the streets! The Minister of Commerce had raised the price of gasoline. In response, the taxi drivers went on strike. The next day the teachers were striking, too. The high school students came out into the streets, attacking and burning buses, and let me mention that His Impeccable Highness owned the bus company. Trying to suppress these pranks, the police catch five high school students, and in a lighthearted mood send them tumbling down a steep hill-side and take potshots at the rolling boys. Three of the boys are killed and two seriously wounded. After this incident come the judgment days: confusion, despair, abuse. In support of the high schoolers, the university students move out for a demonstration, no longer thinking of learning or of grateful diligence, but only of sticking their noses into everything and undermining insolently. Now they are heading straight for the Palace, so the police shoot, club, arrest, and set the dogs on them, but nothing avails, and so to please them, to calm them, His Benevolent Highness recommends calling off the gasoline price rise. But the street doesn't want to calm down!

On top of all this, like a bolt from the blue, comes the news that the Second Division has rebelled in Eritrea. They occupy Asmara, arrest their general, lock up the provincial governor, and make a godless proclamation over the radio. They demand justice, pay raises, and humane funerals. It's tough in Eritrea, sir, where the army fights guerrillas and plenty of people die. The problem of burial had existed for a long time, which is to say that in order to limit excessive war expenses, only officers had a right to a funeral, while the bodies of the common soldiers were left to the vultures and hyenas. Such inequality now caused a rebellion. The following day the navy joins the rebels and its commander, the Emperor's grandson, flees to Djibouti. It is a great distress that a member of the royal family has to save himself in such an undignified, unworthy way. But the avalanche rolls on, my dear sir, because that very day the air force mutinies. Airplanes buzz the city and, according to rumor, drop bombs. The next day our biggest and most important division, the Fourth, rebels and immediately surrounds the capital, demanding a raise and insisting that the ministers and other dignitaries be brought to court because, the soldiers say, they corrupted themselves in an ugly way and should stand in the pillory of public opinion. Well, the Fourth Division's bursting into flames means that the conflagration is close to the Palace and everybody had better save himself quickly. That very night, His Magnanimous Highness announces a pay raise, encourages the soldiers to return to their barracks, urges calm and tranquillity. He himself, concerned about the image of the court, orders Premier Aklilu and his government to offer their resignations —that must have been a hard order for him to give because Aklilu, even though disliked and condemned by the majority, was a great favorite and confidant of the Emperor. At the same time, His Highness raised the dignitary Endelkachew, a person considered a liberal and blessed with a talent for well-turned words, to the post of premier.

## N. L. E.:

At that time I was titular clerk in the computation department of the office of the grand chamberlain of the court. The change of government loaded us down with work, since our department was responsible for supervising the Emperor's instructions on the number of mentions of particular dignitaries and notables. His Highness had to take care of this matter personally, because every dignitary wanted to be mentioned all the time, and as close to His Unrivaled Majesty's name as possible. There was constant quarreling, envy, and intrigue: who is mentioned and who isn't, how many times and in what order. Even though we had strict instructions and norms precisely established by the throne about who is to be mentioned and how many times, such unrestricted greed and freedom arose that we, common clerks, were pressed by the dignitaries to mention them above and beyond the set order, beyond the norms. Mention me, said one and then another, and when you need something you can count on me. Is it surprising, then, that a temptation was born to mention them, in turn, above the limit, and thus gain high-placed patrons for ourselves? The risk was great, however, since adversaries counted how often each of them was mentioned, and if they caught any surplus they immediately lodged an informant's report with His Judicious Highness, who either issued a rebuke or smoothed things over. Finally the grand chamberlain issued an order to introduce cards for the dignitaries, to record the number of times each one was mentioned, and to prepare monthly reports on the basis of which His Benevolent Highness issued additional recommendations about where to subtract and where to add. And now we had to throw away all the cards of the Aklilu cabinet and make up new ones. Special pressures were put on us, since the new ministers strove eagerly to be mentioned and each one tried to take part in receptions and celebrations in order to be mentioned on those occasions.

Very shortly after the change of cabinets, I found myself on the sidewalk because of an incomprehensible and quite unpardonable mental blackout. Once I failed to mention a new minister in the court, Mr. Yohannes Kidane, and he flew into such a rage that, in spite of my appeals for mercy, he had me fired.

## March—April—May

S.:

I don't have to explain to you, my friend, that we were beset by a devilish conspiracy. If it hadn't been for that, the Palace would have stood for a thousand more years, because no Palace falls of its own accord. But what I know now, I didn't know yesterday when we were sliding toward ruin—and, in a stupor, blind, in a hellish state of asphyxiation, confident of our power, exalting in ourselves, we didn't look ahead. And all the while the street agitates without interruption. Everybody is demonstrating—students, workers, Muslims, all demand rights, strike, organize meetings, curse the government. A report comes in about a mutiny in the Third Division, stationed in Ogaden. Now our whole army is in ferment, set against authority, and only the Imperial Guard still shows any loyalty. Because of this insolent anarchy and slanderous agitation, dragging on beyond all tolerance, whispering starts in the Palace. Dignitaries watch each other warily, wondering as they watch. What will happen? What to do? The whole court smothers, crushes, fills itself with rumors, psst-psst here, psst-psst there, and they spend all their time mooning about the corridors, gathering in salons, scheming in secret, organizing meetings, cursing the nation. And the cursing, reproaching, envy, and animosity between the Palace and the street are growing reciprocally, poisoning everything.

I would say that slowly, gradually, three factions appear in the Palace. The first, the Jailers, are a fierce and inflexible coterie who demand the restoration of order and insist on arresting the malcontents, putting them behind bars, beating and hanging them. This faction is led by the Emperor's daughter Tenene Work, a sixty-two-year-old lady permanently cross and obstinate, always reproaching His Ineffable Highness for his kindness. A second faction coalesces, the Talkers, a coterie of liberals: weak people, and philosophizers, who think that one should invite the rebels to sit down at a table and talk, listen to what they say, and improve the Empire. Here the greatest voice is that of Prince Mikael Imru, an open mind, a nature ready for concessions, himself a well-traveled man who knows the developed countries. Finally, the third faction is made up of Floaters, who, I would say, are the most numerous group in the Palace. They don't think at all, but hope that like corks in water they will float on the waves of circumstance, that in the end things will somehow settle down and they will arrive successfully in a hospitable port. And when the court divided itself into the Jailers, the Talkers, and the Floaters, each coterie started voicing its arguments, but voicing them secretly, in the underground manner, because His Highness didn't like factions and hated chattering, applying pressure, and any kind of peace-shattering insistence. Yet for the very reason that the factions appeared and began slinging mud and drawing blood, biting and fighting, grinding their jaws and showing their claws, everything in the Palace came to life for a moment, the old verve returned, and it felt like home again.

L. C.:

In those days His Majesty rose from his bed with ever-increasing difficulty. Night after night he slept badly or not at all, and then he would nod off during the day. He said nothing to us, not even during meals, which he ate surrounded by his family. Only during the reports submitted during the Hour of Informants would he come to life, because his people now brought very interesting news that a conspiracy of officers had arisen in the Fourth Division, with agents placed in all the garrisons and in the police all over the Empire, but who was in that conspiracy the informants could not tell because everything was being done in such secrecy. His Venerable Majesty, said the informants afterward, listened to them eagerly but gave no orders, asked no questions. It astonished them that instead of ordering arrests and hangings, His Majesty walked around the gardens, fed the panthers, set out grain for the birds, and remained silent.

In the middle of April, amid the constant unrest in the streets, His Majesty ordered that the ceremony of the succession be organized. Dignitaries gathered in the great throne chamber, waiting and whispering about whom the Emperor would nominate as his successor. This was a new thing, because His Majesty always used to punish and condemn any sort of rumors or sly comments about the succession. Now obviously moved to the highest degree by the affair, so that his quiet voice cracked and could barely be heard, His Most Gracious Majesty announced that, bearing in mind his advanced age and the ever-more-often-heard call of the Lord of Hosts, he was nominating—after his own pious decease—his grandson Zera Yakob as the successor to his throne. This young man, twenty years old, was studying at Oxford. He was sent out of the country some time before because he was leading too free a life, thus causing great worries to his father, Prince Asfa Wossen, the only remaining son of the Emperor, who lived permanently paralyzed in a Geneva hospital. Even though such was His Majesty's will in the matter of the succession, old dignitaries and venerable members of the Crown Council started to complain and even to protest surreptitiously. They said that they would not serve under such a youngster, because to do so would be a humiliation and an offense to their advanced age and their many merits. Right away an antisuccession faction formed, one that pondered ways to summon the Dame Jailer, Tenene Work, daughter of the Emperor, to the throne. And another faction appeared immediately in favor of bringing to the throne another grandson of the Emperor, the Prince Makonen, who was being educated at an officers' school in America.

And so, my friend, in the middle of these suddenly unleashed succession intrigues that plunged the whole court into such bitter fighting that no one thought about what was going on in the Empire, quite unexpectedly and surprisingly the army enters the town at night and arrests all the ministers of the old Aklilu government. They even lock up Aklilu himself, as well as two hundred generals and high-ranking officers distinguished by their unfaltering loyalty to the Emperor. Nobody has had time to recover his senses after this exceptional blow, when news comes that the conspirators have arrested the chief of the General Staff, General Assefa Ayena, the man most loyal to the Emperor and the man who saved the throne during the December events by destroying the Neway brothers and defeating the Imperial Guard. In the Palace—an atmosphere of terror, fear, confusion, depression. The Jailers are pressing the Emperor to do something, to order the rescue of those who have been imprisoned, to drive away the students, and to hang the conspirators. His Benevolent Majesty hears out all the advice, nods his assent, gives comfort. The Talkers say that it's the last chance to sit down at the table, bring the conspirators around to one's own point of view, and repair and improve the Empire. These, too, His Benevolent Majesty hears out, nodding approval, comforting. Days go by and the conspirators lead first one person, then another, out of the Palace and arrest him. Again the Lady Jailer reproaches His Most Puissant Majesty, saying that he doesn't defend loyal dignitaries. But apparently, my friend, it is the way of the world that the more loyally a person acts, the more of a beating he attracts, because when some faction has him pinned, His Majesty leaves him to twist in the wind. This was something the princess could not comprehend; she wanted to stick with the loyal ones until the bitter end.

May was coming, the last moment to swear in the cabinet of Premier Makonen. However, the Imperial protocol announces that the swearing-in will be difficult because half of the ministers have already been arrested, or have fled abroad, or have stopped coming near the Palace. As for the premier, the students call him names and throw stones at him, because Makonen never knew how to make people like him. Immediately after his promotion he swelled somehow; his gaze became fixed in the distance and so hazed over that he did not recognize anyone. No one could tame him. Some lofty force propelled him through the corridors and made him appear in salons, where he stalked in inaccessible and stalked out unreachable. And wherever he appeared he would start a worship service around himself, for himself. Others kept it going, hosannaing it up, incensing it up, with adoration, incantation, and supplication for mediation. It was already obvious that Makonen could not long remain in power, because neither the soldiers nor the students wanted him. I can't even remember whether the swearing-in finally took place or not, because they kept locking up one minister after another. You must realize, my friend, that the cunning of our conspirators was remarkable. Whenever they arrested someone, they immediately announced that they had done so in the name of the Emperor, and right away they would emphasize their loyalty to His Majesty. This made him very happy, because whenever Tenene Work came to her father to denounce the army, he would scold her, praising the fidelity and devotion of his army. He soon received new proof of this, for in the beginning of May war veterans organized a demonstration of loyalty in front of the Palace, raising their voices in praise of His August Majesty, and the noble monarch came out onto the balcony, thanked his army for its unshakable loyalty, and wished it further prosperity and success.

*June—July*

U. Z.-W.:

In the Palace, dejection, discouragement, fearful waiting for whatever might happen tomorrow—when suddenly His Majesty summons his counselors, reprimands them for neglecting development, and after giving them a scolding announces that we are going to construct dams on the Nile. But how can we erect dams, the confused advisers grumble, when the provinces are starving, the nation is restless, the Talkers are whispering about straightening out the Empire, and the officers are conspiring and rounding up the notables? Immediately, audacious rumors are heard in the corridors saying that it would be better to help the starving and forget about the dams. To this the Finance Minister replies that if the dams are built, it will be possible to let water into the fields and such an abundant harvest will result that there will be no more death from starvation. Well, yes, murmur those who had been whispering, but how long will it take to build the dams? In the meantime the nation will die of hunger. "The nation isn't going to die," explains the Finance Minister. "It hasn't died yet, so it isn't going to die now. And if we don't build the dams," he asks, "how are we going to catch up and surpass?" "But against whom are we supposed to be racing, anyway?" murmur the whisperers. "What do you mean, whom?" says the Finance Minister. "Egypt, of course." "But Egypt, sir, is wealthier than we are, and even Egypt couldn't put up dams out of its own pocket. Where are we supposed to find the funds for our dams?" Here the minister really lost his temper with the doubting, and began lecturing them, telling them how important it is to sacrifice oneself for development. Besides, His Majesty has ordered, has he not, that we all develop constantly, without resting even for a moment, putting our hearts and souls into it. And the Minister of Information immediately announced His Venerable Majesty's decision as a new success, and I remember that in the twinkling of an eye the following slogan appeared in the streets of the capital:

As soon as the work on the dams is done,
Wealth will accrue to everyone!

Let the slanderers spew their lies and shams—
They will suffer in hell for opposing our dams!

Nevertheless, this affair so infuriated the conspiring officers that the Imperial Council established by His Unrivaled Highness for the special purpose of supervising the dams was thrown into jail a few days later, on the grounds that nothing could come of the dams but increased corruption and more starvation among the people. I have always been of the opinion, however, that this action on the part of the officers must have brought particular grief to His Majesty. He felt that the years were burdening his shoulders with an ever-increasing weight, and so he wanted to leave an imposing and universally admired monument after himself. That way, many years hence, everyone who could get to the Imperial Dams would cry out, "Behold, all ye! Who but the Emperor could have caused such things to be done, such extraordinary, wondrous things, whole mountains flung across the river!" Or, to look at it from another angle, were he to give ear to the whispers and murmurs that it would be better to feed the hungry than to build dams . . . well, the hungry, even if they are satiated at last, will eventually die, leaving behind not a trace—neither of themselves, nor of the Emperor.

The one I am talking to ponders for a long time whether the Emperor had already begun to think about his departure. He had appointed his successor to the throne, hadn't he, and ordered the creation of an eternal monument to himself in the form of those dams along the Nile. (How extravagant an idea when juxtaposed with the other, burning needs of the Empire!) However, he thinks there was more to it. In naming his young grandson as his successor to the throne, the Emperor was punishing his son for the disgraceful role he had played in the events of December 1960. By ordering the construction of dams on the Nile, he wanted to prove that the Empire was growing and flourishing and that all the slanders about poverty and corruption were only the malicious chatter of those opposed to monarchy. In reality, the thought of leaving was completely alien to the Emperor's nature; he treated the state as his personal creation and believed that with his departure the country would fall apart and disappear. Was he to annihilate his own creation? Moreover, was he to leave the walls of the Palace and expose himself of his own free will to the blows of enemies who lurked in waiting? No, departure from the Palace could not be considered; instead, after short attacks of senile depression, the Emperor seemed to rise from the dead, become more lively, acquire new vigor, and it was even possible to see pride on his aged face—that he was so fit, had such presence of mind, and remained so masterful.

June came, the month in which the conspirators, having strengthened themselves, finally renewed their cunning attacks against the Palace. Their cunning consisted in this: they carried out all their destruction of the system with the Emperor's name on their lips, as if executing his will and humbly realizing his thoughts. Now—claiming to do so in the name of the Emperor—they created a commission to investigate corruption among dignitaries, checking their accounts, landholdings, and all other riches. The people of the

*Palace were overcome by terror because in a poor country, in which the only source of property is not hard work and productivity but extraordinary privilege, no dignitary could have a clear conscience. The more cowardly ones thought of fleeing abroad, but the military closed the airport and put a ban on leaving the country. A new wave of arrests started. People disappeared from the Palace every night; the court became more and more deserted. A great commotion was caused by news of the imprisonment of Prince Asrate Kassa, who presided over the Crown Council and was, after the Emperor, the most important person in the monarchy. The Minister of Foreign Affairs, Minassie Haile, also found himself in prison, as did over a hundred other dignitaries. At the same time, the army occupied the radio station and announced for the first time that a coordinating committee of the armed forces and the police stood at the head of the movement for renewal, acting—as they kept claiming—in the name of the Emperor.*

C.:

The whole world stood on its head, my friend, because strange signs appeared in the sky. The moon and Jupiter, stopping in the seventh and twelfth houses instead of turning in the direction of the triangle, began ominously to form the figure of a square. Accordingly, the Indians who explained the signs at court now fled the Palace, probably because they were afraid to disturb His Venerable Majesty with a bad omen. But Princess Tenene Work must still have had meetings with these Indians, because she would run through the Palace perturbed, upsetting His August Majesty, urging him to order imprisonments and hangings. And the remaining Jailers also pressed His Noble Majesty—and even begged him on their knees—to stop the conspirators, to put them behind bars. They were completely dumbfounded, however, completely unable to understand, when they saw that His Most Singular Majesty wore his military uniform all the time (medals jingling), and carried his marshall's baton, as if he wanted to show that he still commanded his army, still stood at its head, and still gave the orders. No matter that this army had designs against the Palace. Well, so it had, but under his command it was a faithful, loyal army, which did everything in the Emperor's name. They rebelled? Yes, but they rebelled loyally!

That's it, my friend—His Venerable Majesty wanted to rule over everything. Even if there was a rebellion, he wanted to rule over the rebellion, to command a mutiny, even if it was directed against his own reign. The Jailers murmur that stupor must have come over His Majesty if he can't understand that by acting the way he does he is supervising his own fall. But His Kindly Majesty does not listen to anyone. He receives in the Palace a delegation of that military committee called "Dergue" in the Amharic language, locks himself in his office with the delegation, and starts conferring with the conspirators! At that moment, my friend, I must confess with shame that one could hear godless and reprehensible rumors in the corridors that His Venerable Majesty has lost his mind, because in this delegation there were common corporals and sergeants, and it is unthinkable that His Majesty could sit down at the table with such low soldiery! Today it is difficult to deduce the subject of His Majesty's conference with these people, but immediately afterward new arrests started and the Palace was even more depopulated. They locked up Prince Mesfin Shileshi, a great lord with his own private army, which they immediately disarmed. They imprisoned Prince Worku Selassie, who had immense landholdings. They imprisoned the emperor's son-in-law General Abiye Abebe, the Minister of

Defense. Finally they locked up Premier Endelkachew and several of his ministers. By now they were imprisoning someone every day, insisting that it was in the name of the Emperor.

The Lady Jailer kept urging her venerable father to show some firmness. "Father, stand your ground and unveil your severity!" But, to tell the truth, what sort of firmness can one show at such an advanced age? His Majesty could only use a soft approach now, and he proved his wisdom by displaying a conciliatory attitude instead of trying to overcome the opposition with toughness, intending thus to appease the conspirators. And the more the Lady demanded harshness, the more she regarded his softness with anger, and nothing could calm her or settle her nerves. But His Benevolent Majesty never lost his temper; on the contrary, he always praised her, comforted her, cheered her up. Now conspirators came to the Palace more often, and His Majesty received them, heard them out, praised their loyalty, encouraged them. The Talkers took heart, calling all the time for sitting down at the table, improving the Empire, meeting the demands of the rebels. And whenever the Talkers would present a manifesto in that spirit, His Most Exceptional Majesty would praise them for their loyalty, comfort them, and encourage them. But the Talkers were also being thinned out by the army, so their voices were heard ever more faintly.

The salons, corridors, and galleries grew more deserted each day, and yet nobody took up the defense of the Palace. Nobody gave the call to close the doors and break out the weapons. People looked at one another thinking, Perhaps they'll take him and leave me alone. And if I raise a hue and cry against the rebels, they'll lock me up right away and leave the others in peace. So it's better to keep quiet and not know anything. Better not to leap, in order not to weep. Better to keep your peace, and avoid an early decease.

At times everybody would go to His Highness asking
what to do, and Our Supreme Ruler would listen to our
complaints, praise us, and encourage us. Later on, however,
it became more and more difficult to gain an audience, because His Noble Majesty grew tired of listening to so much
grumbling, demands, and informants' reports. Most willingly he received the ambassadors of foreign countries, and
indeed all sorts of foreign representatives, because they
brought him relief by praising him, comforting him, encouraging him. These ambassadors, along with the conspirators, were the last people with whom His Majesty
talked before his departure, and they confirmed unanimously that he was in good health and had full presence of
mind.

D.:

The remainder of the Jailers, those who were still left in the
Palace, walked through the corridors calling for action. We
must get moving, they said, take the offensive, stand up
against the malcontents. Otherwise everything will perish in
a deplorable way. But how to take the offensive when the
whole court is locked up in defense, how to help if there is
such helplessness, how to listen to the Talkers who call for
change without saying what change? Change could come
only from the monarch. It demanded his support and approval because otherwise it would become faithlessness and
would meet reproof. The same was true of all favors—only
His Majesty could dispense them, and what someone did not
obtain from the throne, he could obtain in no other way.
Thus distress reigned among the courtiers: were His Majesty no longer to exist, who would bestow favors and increase their property?

In this Palace beset by troubles and condemnation, how

very much one wanted to break the passivity, to come up with something worthy, a brilliant flash that would show vigor. Whoever was still fit paced the corridors wrinkling his brow, searching for that thought, straining his head, until finally just such an idea was born: to organize the celebration of an anniversary! "What?" the Talkers cried, "occupy ourselves with an anniversary now? Nonsense. It's the last moment for us to sit down at the table and save the Empire." But the Floaters considered it a worthy, inspirational sign of vitality, and they enthusiastically started to prepare the anniversary, planning all the festivities, including a gala for the poor. The occasion, my friend, was His Majesty's completion of the eighty-second year of his life, though the students started rummaging through some old papers and set up a cry, claiming it was not eighty-two but ninety-two, because, they shouted, His Majesty had once subtracted a few years from his real age. But the students' venom could not poison the holiday that the Minister of Information— miraculously still at large—called a success and the best example of harmony and loyalty. No adversity could overcome this minister, who had such a sharp mind that in the greatest loss he could spot an advantage and turned everything around so cleverly that in failure he saw success, in unhappiness joy, in misery abundance, and in defeat good fortune. Were it not for such turning around, who could have called that sad holiday a wonderful one?

It was raining that day, a chilly rain, and mist floated in the air as His Majesty stepped out onto the balcony to make his speech. Next to him stood only a handful of soaked, depressed dignitaries—the rest were in prison or had fled the capital. There was no crowd, only the Palace servants and some soldiers from the Imperial Guard standing at the edge of an empty courtyard. His August Majesty expressed his compassion for the starving provinces and said that he would not neglect any chance to keep the Empire developing fruitfully. He also thanked the army for its loyalty, praised his subjects, encouraged them and wished them good luck. But he spoke so quietly that through the steady rain one could hardly make out individual words. And know, my friend, that I will take this memory to the grave with me, because I can still hear how His Majesty's voice breaks, and I can see how tears stream down his venerable face. And then, yes, then, for the first time, I thought to myself that everything was really coming to an end. That on this rainy day all life is seeping away, we are covered with cold, clinging fog, and the moon and Jupiter have stopped in the seventh and the twelfth houses to form a square.

All this time—it is the summer of 1974—a great contest is going on between two shrewd antagonists: the venerable Emperor and the young officers from the Dergue. For the officers it is a game of hide-and-seek: they are trying to encircle the ancient monarch in his own Palace, in his lair. And the Emperor? His plan is subtle, but let's wait, because in a moment we will come to know his thoughts.

And other players? The other players of this dramatic and absorbing game are drawn in by the course of events; they know little of what's going on. Helpless and frightened, dignitaries and favorites rampage through the corridors of the Palace. We must remember that the Palace was a nest of mediocrity, a collection of second-rate people, and in a time of crisis such people lose their heads and think of nothing but saving their own skins. Mediocrity is dangerous: when it feels itself threatened it becomes ruthless. Such precisely are the Jailers, who are not up to much beyond cracking the whip and spilling blood. Fear and hatred blind them, and the basest forces prod them to action: meanness, fierce egoism, fear of losing their privileges and being condemned. Dialogue with such people is impossible, senseless. The Talkers are the second group—people of goodwill but defensive by nature, wavering, compliant, and incapable of transcending the patterns of Palace thinking. They get beaten worst of all, from every side, shoved out of the way and destroyed. They try to move about in a context that has been torn in half, in which two extreme adversaries—the Jailers and the rebels—don't want their services and treat them as a flabby, superfluous race, as an obstacle, since extremists tend toward battle rather than reconciliation. Thus the Talkers understand nothing and mean nothing; history has outgrown them and passed them by. About the Floaters nothing can be said. They drift along wherever the current drags them, a school of small-fry carried away, pulled in all directions, fighting, striving for even the meanest kind of survival.

That's the fauna of the Palace, against which the group of young officers is acting—bright, intelligent men, ambitious and embittered patriots conscious of the terrible state of affairs in their fatherland, of the stupidity and helplessness of the elite, of the corruption and depravity, the misery and the humiliating dependence of the country on stronger states. They themselves, as part of the Imperial army, belong to the lower ranks of the elite; they, too, have taken advantage of privileges, so it is not poverty—which they have never experienced directly—that goads them to action, but rather the feeling of moral shame and responsibility. They have weapons, and they decide to make the best use of them. The conspiracy comes into being in the headquarters of the Fourth Division, whose barracks lie in the suburbs of Addis Ababa, actually fairly close to the Emperor's Palace. For a long time the conspirators act in the strictest secrecy —even the slightest suggestive leak could bring repressions and executions. Gradually the conspiracy penetrates other garrisons, and later the ranks of the police.

The event that hastened the confrontation between the army and the Palace was the starvation in the northern provinces. Usually it is said that periodic droughts cause bad crops and therefore starvation. But it is the elites of starving countries that propagate this idea. It is a false idea. The unjust or mistaken allocation of funds and national property is the most frequent source of hunger. There was a lot of grain in Ethiopia, but it had first been hidden by the rich and then thrown on the market at a doubled price, inaccessible to peasants and the poor. Figures about the hundreds of thousands who starved next to abundantly stocked granaries were published. On the orders of local dignitaries, the police finished off whole clans of still-living human skeletons. This situation of intense evil, of horror, of desperate absurdity, became the signal for the conspiring officers to go to work. The mutiny involved all the divisions in turn, and it was probably the army that had been the main prop of Imperial power. After a short period of bewilderment, shock, and hesitation, H. S. began to realize that he was losing his most important instrument.

At the beginning the Dergue acted in darkness, hidden in conspiracy; they didn't know how much of the army would back them. They had workers and students behind them— that was important, but the majority of generals and higher-ranking officers were against the conspirators, and it was the generals who still commanded, still gave the orders. Step by step—that was the tactic of this revolution. If they had come out openly and at once, the disoriented part of the army might have refused to support them or might even have destroyed them. There would have been a repeat performance of the drama of 1960, when the army fired on the army and the Palace was thus preserved for another thirteen years. In any case, the Dergue itself lacked unity; sure, everyone wanted to liquidate the Palace, they wanted to change the anachronistic, worn-out, helplessly vegetating system, but quarrels went on about what to do with the person of the monarch. The Emperor had created around himself a myth, the force and vitality of which it was impossible to ascertain. He was well-liked in the world, full of personal charm, universally respected. What's more, he was the head of the Church, the Chosen One of God, the ruler of men's souls. Raise one's hand against him? It always ended in anathema and the gallows.

The members of the Dergue were people of great courage. And also, to some extent, desperadoes, since they recalled afterward that even when they had decided to stand up against the Emperor, they still didn't believe in their own chances of success. Perhaps H. S. knew something about the doubts and divisions that consumed the Dergue; after all, he possessed an extraordinarily well-developed intelligence service. Perhaps he was guided only by instinct, by his penetrating sense of tactics, by his great experience. And what if it was something else again? What if he simply didn't feel the strength to continue the battle? It seems that he alone, of the whole ruling circle, understood that the wave that had arisen could no longer be withstood. Everything crumbled; his hands were empty. So he began to yield, and more—he stopped ruling. He feigned his existence, but the ones closest to him knew that he really wasn't doing anything; he wasn't in action.

His associates are confused by this inactivity, and they lose themselves in conjectures. First one faction, then the other, presents its arguments to him, each viewpoint at odds with the other. He listens to everyone with the same attention, nods his approval, praises everyone, comforts, and encourages. Haughty, distant, reserved, aloof, he allows events to run their course, as if he were already living in a different space, a different time. Perhaps he wants to stand above the conflict as a means of giving way to the new forces, which he can't stop anyway. Perhaps he reckons that in exchange for this service these new forces will later respect and accept him. Left alone, he, an old man with one foot in the grave, won't be a danger to them, will he? And so he wants to stay? To save himself? The military begin with a small provocation: on charges of corruption, they arrest a few of the already-dismissed ministers from Aklilu's government. They wait anxiously for the Emperor's reaction. But H. S. is silent. That means that the move was successful, the first step taken. Emboldened, they go on—henceforth they put into motion the tactic of gradually dismantling the elite, of slowly and meticulously emptying the Palace. Dignitaries and notables disappear one after the other. Passive, torpid, they await their turn. Later, they all meet in the jail of the Fourth Division, in a new, peculiar, inhospitable anti-

*Palace. In front of the barracks gates, right next to where the Addis Ababa–Djibouti railway line passes, stands a long line of limousines—these are the princesses, the ministers' and generals' wives, shocked and terrified, bringing food and clothing to their incarcerated husbands and brothers, the prisoners of the coming order. A crowd of disturbed and excited spectators gapes at these scenes, because the street doesn't yet know what's going on; it hasn't really got through yet. The Emperor is still in the Palace and the officers are still deliberating in the division headquarters, planning the next move. The great game goes on, but its last act is approaching.*

*August—September*

M. W. Y.:

Amid all the depression, with the sense of being crushed and pushed against a wall—a feeling that filled the Palace and all the courtiers with mournful gloom—there suddenly arrived the Swedish physicians whom His Most Exceptional Majesty had summoned long ago. Delayed by some inexplicable sluggishness they had come only now—to lead calisthenics at court. And please remember, my friend, that things were already in ruins, and whoever hadn't been thrown in the clink was awaiting his hour, stealthily making his covert way through the Palace—afraid to show his face because the rebels were clearing out the place, taking people to prison day and night. No one could slip through a net so tight. And here you were in the middle of all this rounding up and hunting down, and you had to show up for calisthenics! Who on earth can think of calisthenics, the Talkers want to know, when this is the last moment to sit down at the table and put the Empire straight, season it, make it palatable? But it was the desire of His Majesty and the Crown Council, just then, that all the Palace people should take very good care of their health, take full advantage of the blessings of nature, rest as much as necessary in comfort and affluence, breathe good—and preferably foreign—air. His Benevolent Majesty forbade any economizing in this regard, saying often that the life of the Palace people is the greatest treasure of the Empire and the most valuable resource of the monarchy. A decree to just this effect had been issued long before by His Majesty, a decree requiring the performance of these calisthenics, and since the decree was never annulled in spite of the pervasive tumult and growing commotion, we now—we, the last handful of people remaining in the Palace—had to fall in for morning calisthenics and force the greatest treasure of the Empire into supple fitness by moving our arms and our legs about. Since the calisthenics went on, as if to spite the impudent invaders who were slowly taking over the Palace, the Minister of Information called it a success and a heartening proof of the inviolable unity of our court.

The Imperial decree I spoke of also ordered anyone who exerts himself in the slightest in his governmental duties to take a little rest immediately, to go to a secluded and comfortable spot, loosen up, take deep breaths, and, having adorned himself with everyday clothing and made himself casual, to get closer to nature. And anyone who neglected these vacations, whether out of forgetfulness or overzealousness, was scolded by His August Majesty and admonished by other courtiers not to waste the treasure of the Empire, but instead to preserve the most valuable resource of the monarchy. Yet how could you get closer to nature and enjoy your rest if the officers were not letting anyone out of the Palace? If someone managed to sneak home, the rebels would be lying in ambush and seize him and throw him into jail. But the worst thing about the calisthenics was that when a group of courtiers gathered in a salon to wave their arms and legs about, the conspirators would march in and drive everyone off to jail. "People whose days are numbered doing calisthenics!" the officers snickered, making impudent jokes. This was the best proof that the officers had no respect for values and acted against the good of the Empire. Even the Swedish physicians had a fright. Eventually they lost their contracts—though they were lucky to get away with their lives. To prevent the rebels from capturing everyone at once, the grand chamberlain of the court pulled off a cunning trick by ordering that calisthenics be done in small groups. So if some fell into the trap, others would be saved, and having persevered through the worst, they would keep the Palace under their control. However, my friend, not even this cautious and ingenious stratagem helped much in the end, because by then the rebellion had grown arrogant, pounding fiercely at the Palace with a battering ram and persecuting us with exceptional relentlessness.

And so came the month of August, the last weeks of power for our supreme ruler. But do I really express myself well, using the word "power" about those last days of decline? It's so very difficult to establish where the borderline runs between true power that subdues everything, power that creates the world or destroys it—where the borderline is between living power, great, even terrifying, and the appearance of power, the empty pantomime of ruling, being one's own dummy, only playing the role, not seeing the world, not hearing it, merely looking into oneself. And it is still more difficult to say when omnipotence becomes powerlessness; good fortune, adversity; luster, tarnish. That is exactly what no one in the Palace could sense, since all gazes were so fixed that in powerlessness they saw omnipotence, in adversity good fortune, in tarnish luster. And even if someone had a different perception, how could he, without risking his head, fall to the ground at our monarch's feet and say, "Your Majesty, you are already powerless, surrounded by adversity, becoming tarnished!" The problem in the Palace was that we had no access to the truth, and we didn't recover our senses until we were behind prison fences. In each person things were comfortably divided, seeing from thinking, thinking from speaking, and no man had a place for these three faculties to meet and produce an audible voice. But in my eyes, friend, our misfortunes all started when His Most Exceptional Majesty allowed the students to gather at that fashion show and thereby gave them a chance to form a crowd and begin a demonstration, setting off the whole dissent movement. That's where the big mistake was: no movement should have been permitted, since we could exist only in immobility. The more immobile immobility is, the longer and surer its duration. And His Majesty's action was strange because he himself knew this truth very well, which was evident, for example, from the fact that his favorite stone was marble. Marble, with its silent, immobile, painstakingly polished surface, expressed His Majesty's dream that everything around him be immobile and silent, and just as smooth, evenly cut, forever settled, to adorn majesty.

A. G. :

You must know, Mr. Richard, that by early August the inside of the Palace had lost its stateliness and its awe-inspiring solemnity. There was such confusion everywhere that the remaining ceremony officials could not introduce any order. The Palace had become the last refuge for the dignitaries and notables, who came here from the whole Empire, hoping to be safer at His Majesty's side, hoping that the Emperor would save them and obtain their freedom through his entreaties to the arrogant officers. Without respect for their honors and titles, dignitaries and favorites of all ranks, levels, and distinctions now slept side by side on the carpets, sofas, and armchairs, covering themselves with curtains and drapes—over which they got into constant quarrels, since some didn't want the curtains taken down from the windows, for fear the rebellious air force would bomb the Palace if it were not kept blacked out. The others maintained that they couldn't fall asleep without covers (you have to admit that the nights then were exceptionally cold), and they selfishly pulled down the curtains and covered themselves. All these squabbles and gibes were meaningless, however, because the officers soon reconciled everyone by taking them to jail, where the contentious dignitaries couldn't count on any covers.

In those days, patrols from the Fourth Division would come to the Palace every morning. The rebellious officers would get out of their cars and order a meeting of dignitaries in the throne room. "Meeting of dignitaries! Meeting of dignitaries!" the cries of the ceremony officials resounded through the corridors. These officials were already sucking up to the officers. At the sound of this call some of the dignitaries hid in corners, but the rest, wrapped in curtains and drapes, showed up. Then the officers read their list and those whose names had been called were taken to jail.

One must remark, Mr. Richard, that His Majesty was now always dressed in his uniform, sometimes in the ceremonial uniform, sometimes in the field uniform, the battle dress in which he used to watch maneuvers. He would appear in the salons where the terrified dignitaries lay on the carpets and lounged on the sofas, asking each other what fate would descend on them when their waiting came to an end. He would comfort them, wish them success, attach the greatest importance, treat them with personal care. However, if he met a patrol of officers in the corridor, he encouraged them as well, wished them success, thanked the army for its loyalty to him; he assured them that army affairs were the object of his personal care. At this point the Jailers would angrily and venomously whisper that the officers should be hanged because they had destroyed the Empire. The kindly monarch would hear them out attentively, encourage, wish them luck, and thank them for their loyalty, underlining the fact that he valued them highly. And the indefatigable mobility of His Venerable Majesty, by which he contributed to the general welfare, never sparing his advice or directives, was called a success by Mr. Gebre-Egzy, who saw in it proof of the monarchy's resilience. Unfortunately, by calling everything a success, the minister so infuriated the officers that they dragged him from the hall and gagged him once and for all, throwing him in jail.

I lived through the blackest days of that last month as an official in the Ministry of Palace Provisions, Mr. Richard. And let me tell you that it was impossible to ascertain the number of people in our court, since the roster of dignitaries changed every day—some sneaked into the Palace counting on help, others were taken off to jail, and often someone who had sneaked in overnight would be in jail by noon. So I didn't know how much food to order from the warehouses. Sometimes there were too few servings, and the gentlemen dignitaries would have a fit, asserting that the ministry is in collusion with the rebels and wants to break down the court by hunger. On the other hand, if there were too many servings the officers would scold me for letting wastefulness reign at court. So I was planning to offer my resignation, but this gesture proved to be unnecessary since they drove us all out of the Palace anyway.

## Y. Y.:

We were by now only a handful, waiting for the final and most terrible verdict, when—praise be to God!—a ray of hope appeared in the form of the lawyers who at last, after long deliberations, had prepared a revised constitution and come to His Majesty with their proposal. The proposal consisted in changing our autocratic Empire into a constitutional monarchy, creating a strong government and leaving to His Venerable Highness only as much power as the British kings have. The distinguished gentlemen started reading the proposal immediately, dividing into small groups and hiding in secret corners, because whenever the officers noticed a larger gathering they jailed them right away. Unfortunately, my friend, the Jailers opposed this proposal, insisting that absolute monarchy should be preserved, the full power by notables and dignitaries in the provinces maintained, and the delusions about constitutional monarchy, coming as they did from the moribund British Empire, thrown to the dogs. Here, however, the Talkers started jumping down the Jailers' throats, saying that it was the last moment to improve the Empire through constitutional change, season it, make it palatable. And so, quarreling, they went to His Merciful Highness, who was just then receiving the delegation of lawyers and looking into the details of their proposal with personal attention, attaching the greatest importance to their ideas. Now, having listened to the sulking of the Jailers and the flattery of the Talkers, he praised all, encouraged, and wished everyone success. But someone must have run off to the officers and informed, because hardly had the lawyers emerged from His Enlightened Majesty's office when they ran into the military, who immediately snatched the proposal from them, ordered them to go home, and forbade them to return to the Palace.

Life inside the Palace seemed strange, as if existing only

of itself and for itself. When I went to town as an official of the Palace post office, I would see normal life—cars driving through the streets, children playing, people selling and buying, old men sitting, talking away—and every day I would pass from one existence to another, no longer knowing which one was real, and feeling that it was sufficient for me to go into the city, to mingle with the crowds, for the whole Palace to vanish from memory. It would disappear, as if it didn't exist, to the point of making me anxious that when I came back I wouldn't find it there.

E.:

He spent the last days alone in the Palace, with only his old valet de chambre for company. Apparently the group in favor of closing the Palace and dethroning the Emperor had gained the upper hand in the Dergue. None of the names of the officers was known, none was announced—they acted in total secrecy until the end. Now they say that this group was headed by a young major named Mengistu Haile-Mariam. There were other officers, too, but they are all dead. I remember when this Mariam would come to the Palace as a captain. His mother was a servant at the court. I cannot tell who made it possible for him to graduate from the officers' school. Slender, slight, always tense, but in control of himself—anyway, that was the impression he gave. He knew the structure of the court, he knew who was who, he knew whom to arrest and when in order to prevent the Palace from functioning, to make it lose its power and strength, change it into a useless simulacrum that today stands abandoned and deteriorating.

The crucial decisions in the Dergue must have been taken sometime around the first of August. The military committee—that is, the Dergue—was composed of a hundred and twenty delegates elected at meetings in divisions and garrisons. They had a list of five hundred dignitaries and courtiers whom they gradually arrested, creating a sinking emptiness around the Emperor until finally he was left alone in the Palace. The last group, members of the Emperor's inner circle, was jailed in the middle of August. That's when they took the chief of the Imperial bodyguards, Colonel Tassew Wajo; our monarch's aide-de-camp, General Assefa Demissie; the commander of the Imperial Guard, General Tadesse Lemma; the personal secretary to H. S., Solomon Gebre-Mariam; the premier, Endelkachew; the Minister of the Highest Privileges, Admassu Retta; and perhaps twenty others. At the same time they dissolved the Crown Council and other institutions directly subordinate to the Emperor.

Then the officers made detailed searches of the Palace. The most compromising documents were found in the Office of Highest Privileges, and found with all the more ease because Admassu Retta himself started to spill the beans. Once only the monarch distributed privileges, but as the Empire began to fall apart the grabbing and snatching grew so strong among the notables that H. S. was unable to keep things under control, and he handed over some of the distribution of privileges to Admassu Retta. But Admassu Retta was not such a mnemonic genius as the Emperor, who never needed to write anything down, so he kept detailed accounts of his disbursements of land, enterprises, foreign currencies, and the other gratuities given to the dignitaries. All this fell into the hands of the military, who used these gravely compromising documents in a major propaganda campaign about the corruption in the Palace. They awakened anger and hatred in the people. Demonstrations flared up, the street demanded hangings in an atmosphere of horror and apocalypse. It turned out well that the military drove us all from the Palace—maybe that was what saved my head.

## T. W.:

I'll tell you, sir, I knew things were going under just from watching the dignitaries sticking together in a close little pack, slapping each other on the back, telling each other they were right and the rest of the world could go to hell. They didn't even bother to ask us servants for news, because they knew what we said would give them the blues. Anyway, they said, what can we do? Everything's falling apart. And you should have seen the Floaters—all consolation. Everything will work out, they said, because we're in a state of inertia and inertia always wins. We'll hang on in the Palace and the common people will never wake up, they'll never overcome the weight of inertia. If we learn how to give a little here and there, at just the right moments, they'll go on sleeping. We should let sleeping dogs lie. The trick is not to resist evil, but to humor it. And the Floaters might have been right, except for those officers, they had a real burr in their tail, and they just sliced into the Palace, cutting off great hunks of dignitaries, until in the end the Palace was picked clean, flushed out, and there was nobody left except for His Most Extraordinary Majesty and one servant.

*hat servant was the most difficult to find. As old as his former master, he lived buried in such oblivion that when I asked people about him they would shrug their shoulders and say he had died long ago. He served the Emperor until the last day, the moment when the military led the monarch out of the Palace. Then they told the servant to gather up his belongings and go home.*

*In the second half of August the officers arrest the last of H. S.'s circle. They still don't touch the Emperor, because they need time to prepare public opinion: the capital must understand why the monarch is being removed. The officers know about the magical element in popular thinking, and about the dangers it contains. The magical aspect is that the highest one is endowed, often unconsciously, with divine characteristics. The supreme one is wise and noble, unblemished and kindly. Only the dignitaries are bad; they cause all the misery. Moreover, if the one on the top knew what his people were up to, he would immediately repair the damage and life would be better. Unfortunately, these crafty villains pull the wool over their master's eyes, and that is why life is so hard, so low and miserable. This is magical thinking because, in reality, in an autocratic system it is precisely the one on the top who is the primary cause of what happens. He knows what is going on, and if he doesn't know, it's because he doesn't want to know. It was no accident that the majority of the people around the Emperor were mean and servile. Meanness and servility were the conditions of ennoblement, the criteria by which the monarch chose his favorites, rewarded them, bestowed privileges on them. Not one step was taken, not one word said, without his knowledge and consent. Everyone spoke with his voice, even if they said diverse things, because he himself said diverse things. The condition for remaining in the Emperor's circle was practicing the cult of the Emperor, and whoever grew weak and lost eagerness in the practice of this* cult lost his place, dropped out, disappeared. Haile Selassie lived among shadows of himself, for what was the Imperial suite if not a multiplication of the Emperor's shadow? Who were gentlemen like Aklilu, Gebre-Egzy, Admassu Retta, aside from being H. S.'s ministers? Nobodies. But it was precisely such people the Emperor wanted around him. Only they could satisfy his vanity, his self-love, his passion for the stage and the mirror, for gestures and the pedestal.

And now the officers meet the Emperor alone, they confront him face-to-face, the final duel begins. The moment has come for everyone to remove the mask and show his face. This action generates anxiety and tension because the two sides form a new geometry. The Emperor has nothing to gain, but he can still defend himself by his defenselessness, by inactivity, by the unique virtue of occupying the Palace, by virtue of his being long-established—and also because he performed an extraordinary service: he was silent, was he not, when the rebels claimed that they were carrying out the revolution in his name. He never protested, he never called it a lie, and yet it was precisely this charade of loyalty, acted out for months by the military, that made their task so eminently easy. But the officers decide to go further, to follow through to the very end: they want to unmask the deity. In a society so crushed by misery, by privation and worry, nothing will speak more eloquently to the imagination, nothing cause greater unrest, anger, and hatred than the picture of corruption and privilege among the elite. Even an incompetent and sterile government, if it lived a spartan life, could exist for years basking in the esteem of the people. The attitude of the people to the Palace is normally kindhearted and understanding. But all tolerance has its limits, which in its swaggering arrogance the Palace often and easily violates. And the mood of the street changes violently from submission to defiance, from patience to rebelliousness.

Now comes the moment when the officers decide to lay

*bare the King of Kings, to turn his pockets inside out, to reveal to the people the secret hiding places in the Emperor's closet. All the while the ancient H. S. wanders through the deserted Palace, accompanied by his valet, L. M.*

L. M.:

This, my gracious sir, was when they were taking away the last of the dignitaries, inviting the gentlemen to the trucks. An officer tells me to remain with His Venerable Majesty and perform all the services I had always performed. Having said this, he drove away. Immediately I made for the Supreme Office, to lend my ear to the will of His Omnipotent Highness. I found no one in the office. I was walking through the corridors, wondering where my lord had gone, when I discovered him standing in the main reception gallery, watching the soldiers of his Guard loading their backpacks and duffel bags, readying themselves to leave. How can this be? I think—they are all going, leaving His Majesty unprotected in a town full of thieves and unrest. So I go up to them and ask, "And you, my gracious sirs, are you leaving like this, altogether?" "Altogether," they answer, "but the sentry at the gate stays so that if some dignitary tries to sneak into the Palace, they'll capture him." His Venerable Majesty is standing, watching, not saying a word. Then they bow to His Majesty and leave with their bundles, and His Most Reverend Majesty looks on in silence as they go, and in silence he returns to his chamber.

Unfortunately, L. M.'s story is chaotic. The old man cannot turn his images, his experiences, and his expressions into a coherent entity. "Please try to remember more details, father!" urges Teferra Gebrewold. (He calls L. M. "father" because of his age, not of kinship.) So L. M. remembers the following scene: One day he found the Emperor standing in a chamber, looking out the window. He came closer and also looked out the window, and saw cows grazing in the Palace garden. Someone must have told herdsmen that the Emperor is no longer important and that everyone can share his property, or at least the Palace grass.

The Emperor now devoted himself to long periods of meditation ("In this the Hindus once gave him instructions, ordering him to stand on one leg, forbidding him to breathe, making him close his eyes.") Immobile, he would meditate for hours in his office (at least the valet thinks he meditated —perhaps he dozed). L. M. did not dare to disturb him. The rainy season wore on. It rained for days on end; trees stood in water. Mornings were foggy and nights cold. H. S. still wore his uniform, over which he would throw a warm woolen cape. They got up as they had in the old days, as they had for years, at daybreak, and they went to the Palace chapel, where each day L. M. read aloud different verses from the Book of Psalms. "Lord, how they are increased that trouble me! many are they that rise up against me." "Hold up my goings in thy paths, that my footsteps slip not." "Be not far from me; for trouble is near; for there is none to help."

Afterward, H. S. would go to his office and sit down at his desk, on which more than a dozen telephones were perched. All of them silent—perhaps they had been cut off. L. M. would sit by the door, waiting for the bell to ring, summoning him to receive orders from his monarch.

L. M.:

So, my gracious sir, in those days, only the officers intruded.
First they would come to me, asking to be announced to His
Unparalleled Majesty, and then they would enter the office,
where His Highness would seat them in comfortable armchairs. Then they would read a proclamation demanding
that His Benevolent Majesty give back the money that, they
claim, he has been illegally appropriating for fifty years,
depositing in banks around the world and concealing in the
Palace and in the homes of dignitaries and notables. This,
they say, should be returned, because it is the property of
the people, from whose blood and sweat it came. "What
money are you talking about?" His Benevolent Majesty asks.
"Everything went for development, for catching up and surpassing, and the development was proclaimed a success, was
it not? We had no money for ourselves." "Some development!" cry the officers. "All this is empty demagoguery, a
smoke screen." And they get up from the armchairs, lift the
great Persian carpet from the floor, and there under the carpet are rolls of dollar bills stuck together, one next to the
other, so that the floor looked green. In the presence of His
August Majesty they order the sergeants to count the
money, write down the amount, and carry it off to be nationalized.

They leave soon afterward, and His Dignified Majesty
calls me into his office and orders me to hide among his
books the money he used to keep in his desk. Since His
Majesty, as the designated descendant of Solomon, had a
great collection of the Holy Scriptures, translated into many
languages, that's where we stashed the money. Ah, those
officers, clever sharks they were! The following day they
come, read their proclamation, and demand the return of
the money, because, they say, it's needed to buy flour for the
starving. His Majesty, sitting at his desk, shows them the

empty drawers. At which the officers spring from their armchairs, grab all those Bibles from the bookcases, and shake
the dollars out, whereupon the sergeants count them, write
down the figures, and take them away to be nationalized.

All this is nothing, say the officers. The rest of the money
should be returned, especially the amounts in the Swiss and
British banks in His Majesty's private account, estimated
at half a billion dollars. They persuade His Majesty to sign
the appropriate checks, and thus, they claim, the money will
be returned to the nation. "Where am I to come up with all
this money?" asks His Venerable Majesty. "All I have is a
few pennies for the care of my ailing son in a Swiss hospital." "Pretty pennies they are, too," answer the officers, and
they read aloud a letter from the Swiss embassy which says
that His Majesty has on account in banks there the sum of
one hundred million dollars. So they go on quarreling until
finally His Majesty falls into meditation, closes his eyes, and
stops breathing. Then the officers withdraw, promising to
return.

Silence fell on the Palace, but a bad silence, in which one
could hear the shouts from the street. Demonstrators were
marching through the town, all sorts of rabble loitering
about, cursing His Majesty, calling him a thief, wanting to
string him up from a tree. "Crook! Give back our money!"
they cried, "Hang the Emperor! Hang the Emperor!" Then I
would close all the windows in the Palace, to prevent these
indecent and slanderous cries from reaching His Venerable
Majesty's ears, from stirring his blood. And I would quickly
lead my lord to the chapel, which was in the most secluded
place, and to muffle the blasphemous roar, I would read
aloud to him the words of the prophets. "Also take no heed
unto all words that are spoken; lest thou hear thy servant
curse thee." "They are vanity and the work of errors: in the
time of their visitation they shall perish." "Remember, O
Lord, what is come upon us: consider, and behold our re-

proach. The joy of our heart is ceased: our dance is turned into mourning. The crown is fallen from our head: For this our heart is faint; for these things our eyes are dim." "How is the gold become dim! how is the most fine gold changed! the stones of the sanctuary are poured out in the top of every street. They that did feed delicately are desolate in the streets: they that were brought up in scarlet embrace dunghills." "Thou hast seen all their vengeance and all their imaginations against me. Thou hast heard their reproach, O Lord; The lips of those that rose up against me; I am their musick. They have cut off my life in the dungeon, and cast a stone upon me."

And as His August Majesty listened, gracious sir, he would doze off. There I would leave him, proceeding to my lodgings to hear what was being said on the radio. In those days the radio was the only link between the Palace and the Empire.

Everybody listened to the radio then, and those who could afford a television set (still the greatest symbol of luxury in this country) watched. During this period, late August and early September, every day brought an abundance of revelations about the Emperor and the life of the Palace. There was a shower of names and figures, of bank account numbers, of the names of properties and private firms. Dignitaries' houses were shown: the riches gathered there, the contents of secret safes, piles of jewelry. One often heard the voice of the Minister of Highest Privileges, Admassu Retta, who testified before the Commission for Investigating Corruption about which of the dignitaries received what and when, where he himself received it, and what its value was. The difficulty, however, was that it was impossible to determine the borderline between the state budget and the Emperor's private treasury; everything was blurred, muddled, ambiguous. With state money the dignitaries built themselves palaces, bought estates, traveled abroad. The Emperor himself amassed the greatest riches. The older he grew, the greater became his greed, his pitiable cupidity. One could talk about it with sadness and indulgence, were it not for the fact that H. S.—he and his people—took millions from the state treasury amid cemeteries full of people who had died of hunger, cemeteries visible from the windows of the royal Palace.

At the end of August the military proclaimed the nationalization of all the Emperor's Palaces. There were fifteen of them. His private enterprises met the same fate, among them the Saint George Brewery, the Addis Ababa metropolitan bus company, the mineral-water factory in Ambo. The officers kept paying their visits to the Emperor, having long talks with him, urging him to withdraw his money from foreign banks and transfer it to the national treasury. The exact sum in the Emperor's accounts will probably never be *known. The propaganda bulletins spoke of four billion dollars, but this was probably a gross exaggeration. It was rather a matter of hundreds of millions. The insistent demands of the military ended in failure: the Emperor never gave his money to the state, and it remains in foreign banks to this day.*

*L. M. recalls that the officers came to the Palace one day and announced that in the evening the television would show a film that H. S. should watch. The valet passed on this information to the Emperor, and the monarch willingly agreed to fulfill the request of his army. In the evening he sat down in his armchair in front of the television and the program began. They were showing Jonathan Dimbleby's film* Ethiopia: The Unknown Famine. *L. M. assures me that the Emperor watched the film to the end and then became lost in thought. That night, September 11, the servant and his master—two old men in an abandoned Palace—did not sleep, because it was New Year's Eve according to the Ethiopian calendar. For this occasion L. M. lit candles in chandeliers all through the Palace.*

*At daybreak they heard the throbbing of motors and the clank of tank treads on asphalt. Then silence. At six o'clock military trucks pulled up in front of the Palace. Three officers in combat uniforms made their way to the chamber where the Emperor had been since dawn. After a preliminary bow, one of them read the act of dethronement. The text, published later in the press and read over the radio, went as follows: "Even though the people treated the throne in good faith as a symbol of unity, Haile Selassie I took advantage of its authority, dignity, and honor for his own personal ends. As a result, the country found itself in a state of poverty and disintegration. Moreover, an eighty-two-year-old monarch, because of his age, is incapable of meeting his responsibilities. Therefore His Imperial Majesty Haile Selas-*

sie I is being deposed as of September 12, 1974, and power assumed by the Provisional Military Committee. Ethiopia above all!"

The Emperor, standing, heard out the officer's words, and then he expressed his thanks to everyone, stated that the army had never disappointed him, and added that if the revolution is good for the people then he, too, supports the revolution and would not oppose the dethronement. "In that case," said the officer (he was wearing a major's uniform), "His Imperial Majesty will please follow us." "Where to?" H. S. asked. "To a safe place," explained the major. "His Imperial Highness will see." Everybody left the Palace. In the driveway stood a green Volkswagen. Behind the wheel sat an officer, who opened the door and held the front seat, so that the Emperor could get into the back. "You can't be serious!" the Emperor bridled. "I'm supposed to go like this?" It was his only gesture of protest that morning. However, he presently fell silent and sat down in the back seat of the car. The Volkswagen set off, preceded by a jeep full of armed soldiers, with an identical jeep following. It wasn't seven o'clock yet. The curfew was still in force. They were driving through empty streets. With a gesture of his hand, H. S. greeted those few people they passed along the way. Finally the column disappeared through the gates of the Fourth Division barracks.

On the orders of the officers, L. M. packed his belongings in the Palace and then went out into the street with his bundle on his back. He flagged down a passing taxi and had himself driven home, to Jimma Road. Teferra Gebrewold says that two lieutenants came that same day at noon and locked the Palace. One of them put the key into his pocket. They climbed into their jeep and left. Two tanks, which had stood before the Palace gates during the night and been showered with flowers by the people during the day, returned to their base.

# HAILE SELASSIE STILL BELIEVES
# HE IS EMPEROR OF ETHIOPIA

Addis Ababa, February 7, 1975 (Agence France Presse). Imprisoned in the rooms of the Menelik Palace on the hills above Addis Ababa, Haile Selassie is spending the last months of his life surrounded by soldiers. According to eyewitness accounts, these soldiers, as in the best times of the Empire, still bow before the King of Kings. Thanks to such gestures, as a representative of an international aid organization discovered recently when he paid a visit to the Emperor and other prisoners remaining in the Palace, Haile Selassie still believes that he is the Emperor of Ethiopia.

The Negus is in good health, has begun to read a lot—in spite of his years he still reads without glasses—and from time to time gives advice to the soldiers who guard him. It bears mentioning that these soldiers are changed every week, because the aged monarch has retained his gift of winning allies. As in the past, each of the ex-Emperor's days is arranged within the framework of an inviolable program and proceeds according to protocol.

The King of Kings gets up at dawn, attends morning mass, and afterward plunges into his reading. The former supreme ruler still repeats what he said on the day of his deposition: "If the revolution is good for the people, then I am for the revolution."

In the Emperor's old chamber, several meters from the building where Haile Selassie is staying, the ten members of the Dergue hold continuous conferences on saving the revolution. New dangers threaten because of the outbreak of war in Eritrea. Close by, the Emperor's lions, locked in their cages and growling threateningly, demand their daily portion of meat.

On the other side of the Palace, near the building occupied by Haile Selassie, stand lodgings for the former court, where dignitaries and notables await their fates in the basements where they are imprisoned.

---

## The Ethiopian Herald

Addis Ababa, August 28, 1975 (ENA). Yesterday Haile Selassie I, the former Emperor of Ethiopia, died. The cause of death was circulatory failure.

Isak Dinesen
## Letters from Africa 1914–1931 £3.95

These letters were the raw material Isak Dinesen was to translate into her later works, introducing us to someone wno is never mentioned in her memoirs – the young, vulnerable Karen Blixen: the miseries of a failed marriage, her illness, the financial collapse of her coffee plantation, the death of her lover, and her irrepressible spirit.

'Deserves to rank beside other great collections of letters like those of Virginia Woolf, or her much admired Byron' THE TIMES

'Above all else, this collection illuminates Karen Blixen's skill as a writer, but unlike her earlier published work, the letters enable you to see her as herself' LONDON REVIEW OF BOOKS

'A major voice of the century' OBSERVER

Dee Brown
## Bury My Heart at Wounded Knee £3.95

'The white man made us many promises, more than I can remember, but they never kept but one; they promised to take our land, and they took it' *Chief Red Cloud of the Oglala Sioux*

'Damn any man who sympathizes with Indians. I have come to kill Indians, and I believe it is right and honourable to use any means under God's heaven to kill Indians' *Col. John M. Chivington*

This Indian History of the American West tells the red man's side of the story. We see their faces, hear their voices as they strive to prevent the encroachment of miners, ranchers, saloon-keepers and soldiers upon their land, their heritage and, finally, their liberty.

Ved Mehta
**Daddyji/Mamaji** £3.50

'Ved Mehta has produced a fascinating work for all those who delight in India' THE TIMES LITERARY SUPPLEMENT

'An outstanding writer of his generation ... the principle task on which he is now engaged is that of a discovery of India through the portrayal of himself and his antecedents' LISTENER

'A strange alien world, haunted by death and tragedy ... Rich with universal truths ... the resonances cut across the boundaries of nationalities, culture and time' THE TIMES

Maxine Hong Kingston
**The Woman Warrior** £2.50
memoirs of a girlhood among ghosts

In the six years since it was first published and won the US National Book Critics Circle Award, *The Woman Warrior* has become a modern classic.

'Tells more than I ever imagined about the strangeness of being Chinese and a woman' NEW SOCIETY

'An investigation of soul, not landscape, its sources are dream and memory, myth and desire; its crises are the crises of heart in exile from roots that bind and terrorise it ... as fierce as a warrior's voice, and as eloquent as any artist's' NEW YORK TIMES BOOK REVIEW

'Dizzying, elemental, a poem turned into a sword ... reimagining the past with such dark beauty, such precision that you feel you have saddled the Tao dragon' NEW YORK TIMES

'One of the books of the decade' TIME

Michael Foot
**Debts of Honour** £2.50

'He pays these *Debts of Honour* to a variety of incongruous people from Right as well as Left of the political spectrum. No narrow bigot could acknowledge as heroes both Hazlitt and Disraeli, both Bertrand Russell and Lord Beaverbrook. Only a determined eclectic could pay homage both to Sarah, Duchess of Marlborough, and to Jonathan Swift, both to Vicky and to Randolph Churchill' THE TIMES

'One of the best literary and political journalists and essayists of our time' GUARDIAN

'... the enthusiastic essayist, using his command of words to praise his Radical heroes past and present. Here are fourteen of them in all their variety ... The book is packed with delights' A. J. P. TAYLOR, EVENING STANDARD

Michael Herr
**Dispatches** £2.50

DATELINE – KHE SANH ...
'Michael Herr dared to travel to that irrational place and to come back with the worst imaginable news: war thrives because enough men still love it' TIME

'Beyond politics, beyond rhetoric ... its materials are fear and death, hallucination and the burning of souls. It is as if Dante had gone to hell with a cassette recording of Jimi Hendrix and a pocketful of pills; our first rock-and-roll war, stoned murder' NEW YORK TIMES

'The best book I have ever read on men and war in our time' JOHN LE CARRE

Anna Coote and Beatrix Campbell
## Sweet Freedom £1.95
**The Struggle for Women's Liberation**

Towards the end of the 1960s, an uprising began among women which was to become one of the most important political developments of this century. It has penetrated the world of paid employment, the mass media, the unions, parliament, local government and personal relationships. It has changed our vocabulary and our consciousness.

Anna Coote and Beatrix Campbell, both active feminists since the early days of the movement, look at the progress of the women's movement so far and examine the reasons for its achievements and failures. They also provide a powerful strategy for the future of the struggle against women's subordination.

Peter Matthiessen
## The Snow Leopard £2.95
**Winner of the US National Book Award.**

In autumn 1973 Peter Matthiessen and biologist George Schaller made the dangerous 250 mile trek from Katmandu to the Crystal Mountain in Tibet, one of the holiest places in Buddhism. While Schaller studied the Himalayan blue sheep, Matthiessen sought a glimpse of the near-mythical snow leopard, seen by only two westerners in a quarter-century. And as a student of Zen, he wanted to consult the revered Lama of Shey Gompa, who had been in seclusion for years. This is both an exciting epic of wilderness travel, and an inspiring account of a 'journey of the heart'.

'A beautiful book' PAUL THEROUX

'A masterpiece' JOHN HILLABY

## Picador

| | | |
|---|---|---|
| ☐ | **Burning Leaves** | Don Bannister | £2.50p |
| ☐ | **Making Love: The Picador Book of Erotic Verse** | edited by Alan Bold | £1.95p |
| ☐ | **The Tokyo-Montana Express** | Richard Brautigan | £2.50p |
| ☐ | **Bury My Heart at Wounded Knee** | Dee Brown | £3.95p |
| ☐ | **Cities of the Red Night** | William Burroughs | £2.50p |
| ☐ | **The Road to Oxiana** | Robert Byron | £2.50p |
| ☐ | **If on a Winter's Night a Traveller** | Italo Calvino | £2.50p |
| ☐ | **Auto Da Fé** | Elias Canetti | £3.95p |
| ☐ | **Exotic Pleasures** | Peter Carey | £1.95p |
| ☐ | **Chandler Collection Vol. 1** | Raymond Chandler | £2.95p |
| ☐ | **In Patagonia** | Bruce Chatwin | £2.50p |
| ☐ | **Sweet Freedom** | Anna Coote and Beatrix Campbell | £1.95p |
| ☐ | **Crown Jewel** | Ralph de Boissiere | £2.75p |
| ☐ | **Letters from Africa** | Isak Dinesen (Karen Blixen) | £3.95p |
| ☐ | **The Book of Daniel** | E. L. Doctorow | £2.50p |
| ☐ | **Debts of Honour** | Michael Foot | £2.50p |
| ☐ | **One Hundred Years of Solitude** | Gabriel García Márquez | £2.95p |
| ☐ | **Nothing, Doting, Blindness** | Henry Green | £2.95p |
| ☐ | **The Obstacle Race** | Germaine Greer | £5.95p |
| ☐ | **Meetings with Remarkable Men** | Gurdjieff | £2.95p |
| ☐ | **Roots** | Alex Haley | £3.50p |
| ☐ | **The Four Great Novels** | Dashiel Hammett | £3.95p |
| ☐ | **Growth of the Soil** | Knut Hamsun | £2.95p |
| ☐ | **When the Tree Sings** | Stratis Haviaras | £1.95p |
| ☐ | **Dispatches** | Michael Herr | £2.50p |
| ☐ | **Riddley Walker** | Russell Hoban | £2.50p |
| ☐ | **Stories** | Desmond Hogan | £2.50p |
| ☐ | **Three Trapped Tigers** | C. Cabrera Infante | £2.95p |
| ☐ | **Unreliable Memoirs** | Clive James | £1.95p |
| ☐ | **Man and His Symbols** | Carl Jung | £3.95p |
| ☐ | **China Men** | Maxine Hong Kingston | £2.50p |
| ☐ | **Janus: A Summing Up** | Arthur Koestler | £3.50p |
| ☐ | **Memoirs of a Survivor** | Doris Lessing | £2.50p |
| ☐ | **Albert Camus** | Herbert Lottman | £3.95p |
| ☐ | **The Road to Xanadu** | John Livingston Lowes | £1.95p |
| ☐ | **Zany Afternoons** | Bruce McCall | £4.95p |
| ☐ | **The Cement Garden** | Ian McEwan | £1.95p |
| ☐ | **The Serial** | Cyra McFadden | £1.75p |
| ☐ | **McCarthy's List** | Mary Mackey | £1.95p |
| ☐ | **Psychoanalysis: The Impossible Profession** | Janet Malcolm | £1.95p |
| ☐ | **Daddyji/Mamaji** | Ved Mehta | £2.95p |
| ☐ | **Slowly Down the Ganges** | Eric Newby | £2.95p |
| ☐ | **The Snow Leopard** | Peter Matthiessen | £2.95p |

| | | | |
|---|---|---|---|
| ☐ | **History of Rock and Roll** | ed. Jim Miller | £4.95p |
| ☐ | **Lectures on Literature** | Vladimir Nabokov | £3.95p |
| ☐ | **The Best of Myles** | Flann O' Brien | £2.95p |
| ☐ | **Autobiography** | John Cowper Powys | £3.50p |
| ☐ | **Hadrian the Seventh** | Fr. Rolfe (Baron Corvo) | £1.25p |
| ☐ | **On Broadway** | Damon Runyon | £3.50p |
| ☐ | **Midnight's Children** | Salman Rushdie | £3.50p |
| ☐ | **Snowblind** | Robert Sabbag | £1.95p |
| ☐ | **Awakenings** | Oliver Sacks | £3.95p |
| ☐ | **The Fate of the Earth** | Jonathan Schell | £1.95p |
| ☐ | **Street of Crocodiles** | Bruno Schultz | £1.25p |
| ☐ | **Poets in their Youth** | Eileen Simpson | £2.95p |
| ☐ | **Miss Silver's Past** | Josef Skvorecky | £2.50p |
| ☐ | **A Flag for Sunrise** | Robert Stone | £2.50p |
| ☐ | **Visitants** | Randolph Stow | £2.50p |
| ☐ | **Alice Fell** | Emma Tennant | £1.95p |
| ☐ | **The Flute-Player** | D. M. Thomas | £2.25p |
| ☐ | **The Great Shark Hunt** | Hunter S. Thompson | £3.50p |
| ☐ | **The Longest War** | Jacob Timerman | £2.50p |
| ☐ | **Aunt Julia and the Scriptwriter** | Mario Vargas Llosa | £2.95p |
| ☐ | **Female Friends** | Fay Weldon | £2.50p |
| ☐ | **No Particular Place To Go** | Hugo Williams | £1.95p |
| ☐ | **The Outsider** | Colin Wilson | £2.50p |
| ☐ | **Kandy-Kolored Tangerine-Flake Streamline Baby** | Tom Wolfe | £2.25p |
| ☐ | **Mars** | Fritz Zorn | £1.95p |

All these books are available at your local bookshop or newsagent, or can be ordered direct from the publisher. Indicate the number of copies required and fill in the form below 11

.................................................................................................................

Name................................................................................................
(Block letters please)

Address............................................................................................

_____

Send to CS Department, Pan Books Ltd, PO Box 40, Basingstoke, Hants
Please enclose remittance to the value of the cover price plus:
35p for the first book plus 15p per copy for each additional book ordered
to a maximum charge of £1.25 to cover postage and packing
Applicable only in the UK

While every effort is made to keep prices low, it is sometimes
necessary to increase prices at short notice. Pan Books reserve
the right to show on covers and charge new retail prices which
may differ from those advertised in the text or elsewhere